# An Actor's Guide to Corporate Role Play

# An Actor's Guide to Corporate Role Play

## The Best Side-Job for Actors

**SYRUS LOWE**

*methuen* | drama

LONDON • NEW YORK • OXFORD • NEW DELHI • SYDNEY

METHUEN DRAMA
Bloomsbury Publishing Plc
50 Bedford Square, London, WC1B 3DP, UK
1385 Broadway, New York, NY 10018, USA
29 Earlsfort Terrace, Dublin 2, Ireland

BLOOMSBURY, METHUEN DRAMA and the Methuen Drama logo are
trademarks of Bloomsbury Publishing Plc

First published in Great Britain 2024

A catalogue record for this book is available from the British Library.

ISBN:    HB:    978-1-3502-8990-1
         PB:    978-1-3502-8989-5
       ePDF:    978-1-3502-8992-5
      eBook:    978-1-3502-8991-8

Typeset by Integra Software Services Pvt. Ltd.
Printed and bound in Great Britain

To find out more about our authors and books visit www.bloomsbury.com
and sign up for our newsletters.

*This book is dedicated to my fearless,*
*hard-working, joyful Grandmother:*

*Murdiel Joyce Soloman*

*Thank you for everything Granny. I honestly couldn't*
*have done it without you.*

*I love you.*

# CONTENTS

# ABOUT THE AUTHOR

Syrus Lowe is a leader in corporate role play, having worked in the industry for over twenty years for some of the top corporate role play companies. He has delivered hundreds of hours of role play in the UK and worldwide, in person and virtually.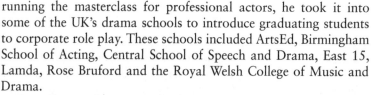

Syrus is part of the audition process for some of the UK's leading role play companies.

In 2016 he set up the first-ever one-day Corporate Role Play Masterclass. As well as running the masterclass for professional actors, he took it into some of the UK's drama schools to introduce graduating students to corporate role play. These schools included ArtsEd, Birmingham School of Acting, Central School of Speech and Drama, East 15, Lamda, Rose Bruford and the Royal Welsh College of Music and Drama.

As well as working as a role play actor, Syrus is now a facilitator, delivering drama-based training on various subjects, including diversity and inclusion, culture change, inclusive leadership, presentation skills and personal impact.

Syrus is a co-founder and CEO of the drama-based diversity, equity, inclusion and belonging training company, The Communication Practice.

Syrus is a RADA trained actor, graduating in 2007, and he sat on the RADA audition panel for five years.

Syrus still works regularly in theatre, film and television. On stage, he was part of the original casts of hit shows *The Inheritance* (Young Vic and West End) and *Best of Enemies* (Young Vic and West End).

His television credits include *Treason* (Netflix), *Strike* (BBC/HBO), *Avenue 5* (HBO), *Protection* (ITV) and *Sherlock* (BBC).

Syrus is also the voice of Lars in the hit *CBeebies* show *Go Jetters*.

# PRAISE FOR SYRUS' CORPORATE ROLE PLAY MASTERCLASS

I had been wanting to dig into corporate role play for a long time, and this masterclass was exactly what I needed! I would highly recommend it to anyone who wants to learn more about the subject. Syrus is a master in this field and talks you through not only the different types of role play and the skills needed but also the practicalities of the industry.

This was a fantastic masterclass; Syrus was incredibly friendly and immediately put the class at ease, providing us with a fun and informative day! His wealth of knowledge and expertise in the world of corporate role play has made me feel confident enough to start writing to different role play companies. I would not hesitate to recommend this masterclass to all actors; I learnt so much in one day – Thanks Syrus!

I've paid for quite a few courses over the last few years – only to be disappointed by the lack of education provided and the overwhelming feeling that I'd been robbed. However – I came away from this masterclass feeling inspired and empowered and have just finished updating my CV to send to all the role play companies on the list provided!

Syrus is a natural teacher and succeeded in making us all feel involved and included – which is no mean feat!

It is a Masterclass, and Syrus is the master at teaching this! You really "get" what corporate role play IS. By the end of the day – one day! – I knew that I could walk into a job and be able to do it. Excellent course.

The masterclass was brilliant, I learnt so much more than I ever thought I would. Syrus was encouraging, knowledgeable, entertaining and very patient—a Saturday very well spent. A must for anyone wanting to get into corporate acting. Thank you Syrus.

Thank you for a brilliant role play Masterclass. I recommend it to anyone interested in working as a role player in the corporate industry. I feel my feedback skills have developed since attending the masterclass. Syrus is generous with his knowledge and experience of all areas of corporate role play.

# ACKNOWLEDGEMENTS

Firstly, I would like to thank the hugely talented actor Babou Ceesay for writing the foreword to this book. Thank you for your time, dedication and honesty. This is a true example of an incredibly successful actor paying it forward with his role play knowledge and sharing how he still uses it in his professional life.

Thank you to all of my colleagues who kindly took the time to provide such detailed and valuable quotes for my book:

Deborah Asante, Amanda Band, Neil Bett, Robert Boulter, Kath Burlinson, Anna Carus-Wilson, Shamia Chalabi, Miles Cherry, Tor Clark, Kate Copeland, Shelley Davenport, Martin Delaney, Abi Eniola, Ali Hendry-Ballard, Alim Jadavji, Alison Johnston, Claire Lichie, Rina Mahoney, Justin McCarron, Pooja Middleton, Julia Montague, Michelle Morris, Louise-Mai Newberry, Mason Philips, Antony Quinn, my friends at RPFT, Mitesh Soni, Carrie Stockton, Victoria Strachan, Abraham Tiyamiyu, Lizzie Twells, Charlie Walker-Wise, Dr JooBee Yeow.

I want to thank all the role players, facilitators and trainers I have worked with. Thank you for your generosity of spirit and for making every day a school day.

I would also like to thank the brave delegates, participants and clients I have worked with over the years. Thank you for trusting me and for your good humour.

Thank you to my brilliant acting agent, Jess Alford, at United Agents Ltd, who is the best. Thank you also to Jess' associate agent, the wonderful Ellie Blackford.

I would also like to thank my writing agent at United Agents Ltd, Zoe Ross and her assistant Oilvia Davies.

I am so grateful for the encouragement and care I have received from my publisher Anna Brewer, and her team at Methuen Drama and Bloomsbury Publishing. Thank you so so much for believing in me and in this endeavor.

Thank you to the incredibly kind Rob Ostlere for your openness, assistance and advice regarding this project.

Thank you to Jill Knight for giving my words a once over on more than one occasion.

And finally, thank you to Lee Knight for your constant support and encouragement.

# FOREWORD

When Syrus approached me about writing the foreword to this book, I immediately jumped at the opportunity. Partly it's my ego; let's face it, who doesn't want to be asked to write a foreword? Well, maybe not everyone. However, the main reason is that I know how valuable this book will be for countless actors, role play companies and, by proxy, corporate clients. It has been a long time coming, and I am glad that Syrus, an excellent actor, role player and facilitator, has taken on the task.

I want to start with a story. It was late 2004 I got a call from a corporate role play company whose name I genuinely don't remember. Another actor had given them my details, and they needed someone to role play a few scenarios with a client. I had heard of role play before; I had even been given the names of a few role play companies to contact; however, I could not make head or tail of most of what was being said on the phone.

I blindly said yes the moment they mentioned how much they would pay me for the day, which was more than I was making a week in my part-time job. There wasn't a brief. I wouldn't have known what a brief was anyway, so I was unlikely to have asked for one. It was also short notice, so the next day I found myself in sunny Reading trying to figure out my way to the location. Fortunately, I got there on time and had gone to the trouble of wearing a suit, a decision I made thirty minutes before leaving my bedsit.

I walked into the room and was met by the facilitator. They quickly explained to me that the client was doing assessments of certain staff members, and I was playing an employee that would be given 'challenging' feedback by said staff members. I had the wherewithal to ask what was required of me. The facilitator explained that I basically needed to 'be in the moment' and 'respond appropriately'. I wanted to press further and ask what type of character I was playing. Any actor worth their salt understands that 'react appropriately' depends on the personality of the person reacting. But I had not yet done years of corporate roleplay and hadn't developed one of the greatest side effects it had on my persona: I had not yet developed my assertiveness.

An hour later, I am sitting opposite the candidate. They are sobbing. I 'reacted appropriately' to being told off by them for a full minute. I got defensive, very. As it happens, I should have become forlorn and dejected. Through their sobs, I could make out 'It is a set-up', 'You brought this guy here to trip me up', and other statements in a similar vein. I felt only marginally better than they did. I felt wretched and exposed. And I felt an immense amount of guilt. Looking around the room, I couldn't help but agree with them. This did indeed feel like a set-up.

It would take a full eighteen months and much cajoling by friends living their best role play lives before I developed the courage to get back on the horse.

If I'd had the chance to read Syrus' incredible book all those years back, I can tell you that this story would have gone a different way.

After a decade of working in corporate role play, I have no doubts about its value. Done properly, it can have a profound impact on everyone involved. As a role play actor, I quickly learned it was not about me. I was there to do what was required of me to support someone else's growth journey.

Now, it's true that it isn't about you; however, I have acquired many skills and much personal growth from my years in the industry.

I've already mentioned assertiveness. Honestly, if you do corporate role play for no other reason, do it to develop your assertiveness, an invaluable asset to have as a human.

There is the obvious financial benefit to being a corporate role player, not to mention the week I got to go to Trinidad. The other unexpected benefit is its impact on my acting skills. For instance, through a type of role play Syrus refers to as bespoke role play, I received a training in character work that would rival any drama school. It was simple – I sat in a room with five candidates and a facilitator. Each candidate had a 'difficult conversation' they wanted to practise. They each had a sheet of paper where they would answer questions about the person they wanted to have said difficult conversation with. Including questions like 'What kind of thing would this person say after a few drinks at the bar'. My job was to get the information off that piece of paper and bring that 'character' to life. I agree with Syrus; it was not about me; however, I always loved the moment a candidate would stop mid-role play and say, 'They are just like that.'

Finally, and above all, the greatest gift that role play gives an actor is the development of their communication skills. Most actors are naturally good communicators; however, what role play does is hone your listening skills. That listening and awareness become invaluable to you as an actor, whether performing or dealing with the industry, but on a much deeper level, as a person. I use the skills I developed doing role play every single day.

As side hustles go, I don't think there is a better job out there for an actor. So, read Syrus' brilliant book, and go forth with confidence into the role play world.

–Babou Ceesay

# Introduction

Welcome to the wonderful world of corporate role play. Firstly, thank you for choosing my book to guide you through this journey. I think I can say with some confidence that if you fully absorb all of the hints, tips and guidance that I provide, you will be well on your way to becoming a great corporate role play actor – using the skills you already have as an actor to get the most out of this rewarding and potentially lucrative field of work.

**Please pay close attention to the activities I ask you to practise in your daily lives to develop your role playing and feedback skills.**

This book will tell you how to do corporate role play, but it will also take you through every stage of entering the corporate role play world. From contacting the role play companies to role play auditions to your first role play job. The more role play work you do, the more skilled you become, job by job. I am a prime example of this. Many of the skills and techniques I will share with you I had to learn on the job. You won't have to do that, as you now have me, this book, and, I believe, a massive head start.

In 2016 I created my Corporate Role Play Masterclass to bridge the gap between actors and role play companies, for actors who felt that the role play industry was impossible to enter and wanted to learn the necessary skills. Also, role play companies who wished to find fresh talent, but time and budget constraints often hampered their recruitment efforts.

This book seemed like the logical next step for me to share my knowledge and expertise with even more of you.

My career as a role play actor began in the best place to learn anything: school. To be more precise, the schools of Newham in East London. There we used role play, more specifically, a type of role play called forum theatre, to tackle the important issues of the day, including bullying, sexual orientation and gender stereotypes. This work was rewarding, and, as you can imagine, the young people would let us know very quickly if we ever began to bore or, worse, patronize them.

I then grew up in character, as it were, and began to act in role play scenarios with local councils, fire services and several police forces.

At twenty-three, I decided to attend drama school to hone my craft. Three years were spent at the Royal Academy of Dramatic Art, after which I graduated with an agent, ready to conquer the industry. As my trusted talent and I chipped away, I fell back on my old friend role play to earn money between acting jobs.

This stage of my role play career saw me working in almost every corner of the economy: finance, government, media, retail and military. You name it, I've sat opposite them.

Corporate role play is now the only job I do alongside acting. This didn't happen overnight. It took many years of hard work and nurturing of relationships. If you are willing to put the work in and are in it for the long haul, I believe you can also get to this place.

I have worked and continue to work with fantastic role play actors, role play companies, facilitators and clients. I have included a selection of thoughts from some of these brilliant people throughout this book.

Enjoy, absorb and see you on the other side.

Syrus :-)

'I stumbled into the world of role play by complete fluke. A friend of mine had a job and needed cover so I said I'd do it. I had no idea how much my world was about to change. After just one job, I realised the power of role play. How I could genuinely impact someone and change the way they behave and bring their best self to work. I've been doing it for seventeen years now, and my only complaint is that I wish I'd discovered it sooner!'

Pooja Middleton
Actor Facilitator

# PART ONE

# WHAT IS IT?

# CHAPTER ONE

# What is corporate role play?

Corporate role play is a process in which people who work in business practise their communication skills with professional actors. Corporate role play allows business people to rehearse and practise the skills needed for high-stakes conversations. That might be a conversation where they have to give someone feedback, fire someone, conduct a medical exam or interview a witness.

The luxury of a rehearsal room is something that we actors can take for granted, where we get to try things and throw them out if they are not working for us. A corporate role play environment gives the business person, sometimes called the delegate, participant or candidate, the freedom of a rehearsal room – the opportunity to practise a conversation, get it wrong or mess it up in a safe space. Throughout this book, I will use all three terms (delegate, participant and candidate) when referring to the business person.

'Role play is now firmly established in mainstream learning and development. When we began, it was often viewed as whacky, at best. At worst, it was viewed with disdain – and by many in the acting profession. I remember being yelled at by a consultant at Guy's Hospital: "Do you have any idea what it's like to have your fate decided by an actor?" It was not a compliment. Recently, a senior civil servant told me the course she had just attended, on emotional intelligence, lacked the transformative input of professional role players.

Corporate role play closes the gulf between theory and practice.'

Abi Eniola
Facilitator and Coach

If you ask a friend or relative, most of them will have done some form of (in their minds) the dreaded 'role play'. I have been in quite a few training rooms where the first thing out of a delegate's mouth is, '*Please say we're not doing any role play today*', or '*I had a sleepless night last worrying that we will be doing role play today.*' Most people have been scarred by role play because their previous experience is often role playing opposite their colleagues. This is not very productive and isn't the best environment for this type of experiential learning. Mainly because you usually have two self-conscious people 'acting' opposite each other. Also, the fact that they are colleagues, usually with much history, comes with its own challenges. This is not an issue when they role play opposite the new face of a talented, neutral actor.

Corporate role play goes by many names: role play, simulation, drama-based learning, drama-based training, business acting, business role play and scenario-based learning, but they all essentially mean the same thing.

Corporate role play falls into two categories: **Assessment and Training.**

## Assessment role plays

This is where a facilitator, examiner or trainer assesses the participant while the participant is doing the role play opposite the actor. They will be assessing several things, including the participant's communication skills. Medical exams and job and promotional interviews are typical examples of assessment role plays.

## Training role plays

Training role plays aim to develop the business person's communication skills. It is generally the same process as assessment role plays, apart from being assessed. This typically means that it is a more relaxed environment as the participant is usually less nervous than if it were an assessment role play. Again, actors are used for this type of role play, as they are communication experts.

It is also worth saying now that the term 'role play' is rapidly going out of fashion. Because of the bad connotations I mentioned previously and also because it implies that the business person needs to 'act'. I know that they technically are during a role play, but the idea of them acting can become a barrier for them and get in the way of their learning. When role playing, I always tell participants to let me worry about the acting part; they are just being themselves practising a conversation.

The more popular (and I think more helpful) term for role play now is 'practice'. It stops the business person from worrying about being a 'good actor'. It also allows them to focus on the valuable learning opportunity of practising a conversation with a neutral professional actor and getting valuable feedback on their communication skills.

'Drama-based training has experienced significant growth and transformation since RPFT was founded in 1988 as "Role Plays for Training". Attitudes and language have progressed (we now prefer the term "skills practice" to "role play"), but the premise remains the same.

If you are new to this line of work, we recommend immersing yourself in the world of Learning & Development to understand what practice-based learning involves and the various tools and techniques we employ. Conduct thorough research, explore resources online and delve into topics like psychometrics, behavioural models and experiential learning.

At RPFT, we prioritise intersectionality and inclusivity when recruiting in order to represent and celebrate the vibrant diversity of the world of work. The best business actors are responsive, excellent at listening and focused fully on the learner. It's interesting and rewarding work, which can fit well alongside a career on stage and screen.'

RPFT

# CHAPTER TWO

# What is a corporate role play actor?

A corporate role play actor plays the person interacting with the business person, such as the employee receiving feedback or getting fired, the medical patient or the interviewed witness.

During the role play, the actor will always be responding, in the moment, to what the business person says and does to them. This will always be an improvisation.

Before any corporate role play job, the role play company sends the actor a briefing document containing the role play scenario and information on the character they will be playing.

The briefing document may contain prompts for the actor, such as:

> *In the role play, if the delegate sensitively and carefully asks about your reasons for being late for work, you will open up and tell them that you are now caring for a sick parent and are struggling to juggle your work and home life at the moment.*
>
> *If they don't ask you any questions but tell you off for being late and issue you with a verbal warning, you will become defensive, monosyllabic and disengaged.*

There is a type of corporate role play called Forum Theatre, where the actor may work with a script, but this would usually be opposite other actors and not delegates.

'I'd invite you to shoo away complacency in this work. It's your worst enemy. Every job needs to be treated like the first job.

If it's your tenth outing of a roleplay on an assessment centre, remember it is the delegates first time. Like telling the story in a play, find your reset button. Find it anew, every time.

The tools and techniques delivered through corporate role play transform other people's life; they enhance conversations, giving them a safer space, a "container" if you like to practice without consequence.'

Victoria Strachan
Behavioural Coach and Facilitator

# CHAPTER THREE

# What is a facilitator?

When working as a corporate role play actor, your 'boss' on the day is usually the facilitator, who runs the day, manages the timings and facilitates the role plays and the following feedback sessions. They will usually already have a relationship with the client and possibly the delegates.

Your role play briefs will always contain learning objectives and the specific communication skills the participant will practise. One of the facilitator's jobs is to give the participant feedback on these particular areas. The facilitator will be a specialist, thus, be very experienced in analysing these areas of communication. They will also be observing the role play from the outside. This gives them a more significant opportunity to observe the delegate and provide detailed feedback. Your focus will, and should, be on doing the role play opposite the delegate, and with the best will in the world, you will only be able to provide a limited amount of feedback, which is fine. Refrain from getting caught up worrying as to why you can't give the type of feedback the facilitator does; your job is only to provide feedback on how you felt during the role play.

The facilitator may have also worked with the delegates for a few hours or days before you arrived, delivering other training elements. This means they will know the group of delegates and their communication styles and challenges very well.

'For experiential learning to take place, as a Facilitator I rely heavily on an actor's intelligence. A good business actor has learned to walk a fine line between understanding the character/role and delivering just the right amount of challenge and reward. A good Business Actor learns to see clearly where the stretch might be for the participant and gently ramps up or down their character's behaviour in order to see how the participant responds in service of their learning. And a good Business Actor knows how to reward.'

Alison Johnston
Facilitator and Executive Coach

It is worth noting that each facilitator has their own approach and style and will want to run their session in a certain way. Make sure you check in with your facilitator at the start of the day to clarify what they require of you as one of their role play actors. Good facilitators mould their sessions to the needs of the delegates in the room, which may mean they may change their minds in the moment and decide to do a different exercise. To be clear, they should never ask you to do something out of your area of expertise, but they may ask you to demonstrate or assist them. For example, the group may be discussing what closed body language looks like, and the facilitator may ask you to demonstrate this physically.

'Facilitators all work slightly differently, so I always like to check in with what they want, how and when they want it. Ultimately, we're there to be helpful to the client and enable the delegates to learn, so be amenable and flexible.

If I'm facilitating I like my role play actors to be on time, well-prepared, calm and professional. No drama in the training room please, unless it's written into the scenario.

I also want my actors to be engaged. I know that the work can get a bit dull and repetitive, particularly if you're lucky enough to be on a roll-out. But remember that you're lucky you've got all this work, so do it to a professional standard. Also remember that while you might have seen this scenario or this coaching model hundreds of times, the delegates haven't. It's your responsibility to guide their attention and awareness towards the materials to support their learning – and not to be at all distracting by being on your phone or looking bored.'

Louise-Mai Newberry
Actor Facilitator

When you work with good facilitators, absorb their temperament, tone of voice, and language as much as possible. That is what I did, and I consider myself a good, empathetic, fun and brave facilitator because of the brilliant facilitators I spent many hours working alongside and observing. If a facilitator uses terminology or refers to communication models which are new to you, ask them for more information after the session or follow the session up with some online research.

In medical role plays you usually have a medically trained examiner in the room with you rather than a facilitator. In some organizations, such as social services or the police force, you may have an in-house trainer rather than a facilitator. Regardless of the title, they all do the same job in their particular setting.

As you progress in your role play career, you may move into the role of Actor Facilitator. An actor facilitator is still a role play actor but takes on some facilitation duties, ultimately assisting the main facilitator. They may also act as the primary facilitator and role player with a small group of delegates in a break-out room. In this instance, they will role play with each delegate and manage the feedback session afterwards. This type of session requires them to provide feedback as the role player and then manage feedback from the delegate and potentially the other delegates who observed the role play.

'The Role of an Actor Facilitator:

You're both guiding and part of the process. Your role is to make participants feel safe enough to practice and have a good learning experience. It helps if, as the facilitator, you're aware of some models of communication you can share with them. The focus is on their learning needs, which may differ for each individual. Contracting is key to helping the participants feel at ease. It helps you establish credibility and trust.

Tip: Have a clear mechanism for when you're in and out of role; for people experiencing this type of learning for the first time, it can be confusing.'

Deborah Asante
Facilitator and Coach

# CHAPTER FOUR

# What is a role play company?

A role play company is like your agent, in the sense that they are the link between you and the client. The role play company will actively find new clients and new work streams. They may also have long-standing clients who repeatedly use them and their team of role play actors. The role play company pay you your fee and charge the client a higher price. This ensures that they make a profit and cover the cost of the work they have to do, such as administrative duties, client meetings, accounting, scripting, and designing role play briefs. Usually, much work will have gone into a role play job over an extended period before the actual role play delivery day.

Different from your agent, the cut the role play company takes is not a standard percentage or one you are even told. Most companies, including role play companies, do not discuss their profit margins with those outside the company.

> For example, a role play company charges the client £375 for one actor for one day.
> The role play company pays you £250 for the day's work.
> The role play company take a third and make a profit of £125.

This may seem like a lot, and as I said, it can vary, but remember that much work will have gone into the set-up and design of that day before you arrive.

Technically, you are not employed by the role play company. They are engaging your services as a freelance, self-employed role play actor. This means that they are not obliged to provide you with work.

You are also responsible for paying your own taxes and national insurance; and will not receive holiday pay or be enrolled on a pension scheme. If you want more information regarding this aspect, speak to your accountant or your country's government tax services.

Unlike your agent, you don't only need to work for or be represented by one role play company. If you're in enough demand, you can work for as many role play companies as you like. After twenty years in the business, I work for around eight role play companies: some a few times a month, others only a few times a year.

One role play company may have an office and a staff of twenty, or they may be one person working from their living room. They may also have diverse clients from many industries or focus on one sector.

Role play companies can offer you work in a variety of ways. Mostly it will be via email like this:

Hi Syrus,

I hope all is well.

Barclays Bank has asked us to provide a team of actors for the Change 100 Programme. The details are as follows:

Date: Tuesday 12th November 2024

Timings: 09.00 arrival for a 09.30 start and finish at 15.00

Contact: Melissa Hartnett (07987343234)

Location: Barclays Bank, 1 Churchill Place, Canary Wharf, London, E14 5RB

Fee: £250 plus travel (lunch will be provided)

You will work alongside one of their in-house facilitators and do six twenty-minute role plays throughout the day.

You will be required to provide feedback to the participants after each role play.

Role play brief to follow. This job is confirmed.

Let me know if you are interested and available.

Kind regards,

Role Play Company

It could also be via a short SMS or WhatsApp message:

> 'Hey Syrus, Are you free for a role play job in London on 12th Nov? 9-3. Barclays Bank. £250. Let me know.'

Sometimes the job will have been confirmed by the client, and sometimes it will be a tentative booking, which we call a 'pencil', much like in the world of commercials. The role play company should clarify when they offer you the job, whether it is confirmed or a pencil. If they don't, then ask.

Your briefing document and any other required material will come to you from the role play company.

There are role play colleagues of mine who are sometimes booked directly by the client. This has never happened to me. I also know that a few of London's hospitals employ their medical role players directly rather than via a role play company.

> 'For me, the main difference between being an actor and a role-player is the use of the "third eye". As actors, we are encouraged to "be fully present", to lock eyes with our scene partner and be unaware of everything else. As role players, we need to be present in a different way. Role Players should be aware of learning outcomes when developing delegates, or, in an assessment centre, creating opportunities for candidates to demonstrate skills and ensuring continuity for all.'
>
> Rina Mahoney
> Actor/Role Player/Coach

# CHAPTER FIVE

# Who uses role play actors?

Many industries in the world use role play and role play actors. Learning and Development (L&D) and Human Resources (HR) departments began to realize that people do not learn by being shown endless PowerPoint Presentations or bombarded with yet another communication model. Or, dare I say it, watching a badly acted training film starring me! Trust me: they are out there!

People learn by doing, experiencing and feeling, by being in the hot seat, as it were. The correct term is 'Experiential Learning', the process of learning by experiencing.

As actors, we are familiar with this because of our experience with the rehearsal process. The more we do it, the more it becomes second nature, and the more natural it begins to feel. Participants experience this when taking part in a role play. Even if, in the beginning, they protest how weird or unreal the experience is, by the end, they are usually fully invested. They will always remember the physiological feeling of being in that chair, opposite you, doing that role play. Of course, providing a group of professional actors for a training session is considerably more expensive than playing a ten-year-old film. The business world values what we do, the skills we bring and the lasting impact our work can have on the culture and behaviours within an organization. I have been in countless sessions where the feedback from delegates has been that the role play element was the best form of training they have ever experienced. I have heard the phrase 'life-changing' used on more than one occasion.

Recently I had the good fortune to watch another actor working through a case play with a delegate.

Later, during the break, the delegate told me how worried she had been about the practice, that it really was a difficult conversation, how vulnerable she felt.

And, that she had felt listened to, gently stretched, and supported.

More importantly, that she felt the kindness of the experience.'

So from the fabulous Maya Angelou:

'I've learned that people will forget what you said, people will forget what you did, but people will never forget how you made them feel.'

Anna Carus-Wilson
Partner with Neil Bett of Frank Partners LLP

During the financial crash of 2008, there was a fear that businesses would stop using actors for role play as they might be deemed too expensive. For a brief period, there was some evidence of this happening. I heard of medical exams replacing role play actors with actual patients; this did not last long. Medical role play days are incredibly long and require great consistency. Some real patients got bored, either leaving early or deviating from their role play briefs and embellishing their illnesses. Not what you need when assessing the next generation of doctors. As I said, this didn't last long, and the actors and the skills they brought were welcomed back with open arms.

The role play industry again felt this concern at the start of the COVID-19 pandemic in 2020. The industry was worried that with a global recession, businesses might find more economical ways of training their workforce. Thankfully, as happened in 2008, the value of what actors do and bring was appreciated. This appreciation and the fact that you can now conduct role plays virtually saved the day, showing the business world again that actors are experts in communication, whether in person or online.

# CHAPTER SIX

# Why do they use actors for role play?

Why spend good corporate pounds, dollars or yen on you? Why pay for your time, travel and (sometimes) lunch when they could get Jim from Accounts or Sandra from Procurement to do the role plays?

Firstly, because actors are brilliant, sensitive shapeshifters. We also bring critical skills that those without our training and experience do not possess.

## Consistency

Consistency is essential for all forms of acting, whether on stage, on screen or in a studio.

Being consistent throughout your role plays is imperative, especially during assessment role plays. Should you not be, you could give a participant an unfair advantage or disadvantage. You must provide each candidate with the same opportunity. You effectively start from the same place each time and let the participant's communicative behaviour influence your behaviour. If you are very emotional and challenging in the morning role plays, then peter out in the afternoon, it will not be fair on the morning participants as you have effectively made it easier for those assessed in the afternoon. Starting from the same emotional state or having an opening line you deliver in the same tone each time is a great way to keep yourself consistent. Some role play briefs will instruct you as to what your opening line of the role play should be.

## Sticking to the brief

Actors are used to learning sacred texts where they must obey every comma and full stop. Role play briefs differ from this, but a team of people will have spent much time ensuring they are 100 per cent correct for that industry, client and participant. The briefs will contain several communication skills the participant must demonstrate when interacting with the role player.

Let's say that the role play brief asks you to, and you do not, hit a certain point, say a specific line or bring up a particular subject; you may make it impossible for the facilitator to do their job and assess the participant in that area. As I said earlier, some of these role plays can decide whether someone gets a job, is made redundant or becomes a doctor. In these instances, the stakes are very high. This may sound scary, but you can't go wrong if you do your prep work and know the brief inside out.

## Real emotion

As actors, we constantly endeavour to connect emotionally to a particular moment and respond in the most truthful way possible. I have been mid-role play before when the emotional place I have gone to has surprised me, but it was only because of how I was impacted by what the participant said or did to me.

A handful of times, participants have had bad reactions to my presented emotion, with them shaking, crying or leaving the room. Never pleasant, but it is a massive part of their learning journey. During the feedback session, I give them a big smile and let them know that I am no longer the role play character but nice friendly role play actor, Syrus. As upsetting as their reaction may have been for them, in that moment, they often share that they also know that the experience will be massively helpful for developing their communication skills moving forward.

# Fearlessness

I played many children during my early years as a role play actor. I was often playing children who had been abused or neglected by the welfare system. The role play briefs would go into extreme detail and were sometimes upsetting as they often were based on real-life cases. No matter how troubling, I had to deliver the role play and play the character without judgement or fear. Playing that character truthfully was a crucial part of the participants learning, and I had to do it justice. These role plays were often with police officers on a training course that would eventually lead to them interviewing real children -- another example of why it is essential to play these characters truthfully, thus providing the correct learning and development experience for the police officer. Many role play briefs can stretch you in this way and benefit your development as an actor. Some examples of other high-intensity role plays can include playing a victim of sexual assault, receiving the news that a relative or partner has died or that you have an incurable illness. You should always be fully aware of the subject of a role play brief before you accept a job.

I have turned down role play jobs because the subject was too close to something I, or someone close to me, had recently experienced. Role play companies will understand this type of response and will never hold it against you. Role play companies are also improving at informing potential role players of any offensive or triggering content contained within a brief when offering role play jobs. My company's work, The Communication Practice, focuses on equity, diversity, inclusion and belonging. Some of our role play briefs, by necessity, may contain racist, sexist, ageist or homophobic language; I will always advise a role play actor of this when I offer them a job.

'I am a staunch advocate of incorporating actor facilitators in the leadership training I design. This approach creates a safe environment for participants to engage in realistic scenarios and explore diverse approaches. It offers remarkable advantages to the participants. Firstly, it allows them to practice and hone the skills required to handle challenging situations effectively. Moreover, this experiential learning instils confidence in individuals when faced with real-life scenarios, enabling them to navigate complexities with the skills they have developed. By immersing participants in simulated real-life scenarios through actor facilitators, leadership training becomes a transformative experience, equipping them with invaluable skills and tools to apply back to the work environment.'

Dr JooBee Yeow
Learngility

# Confidentiality

As actors, we are used to having to keep projects secret. Role play briefs may contain confidential or commercially sensitive information. The role play company may ask you to shred paperwork or delete emails about a particular project. It's rare, but it does happen.

Equally, some raw and sensitive things may come up in the actual role play session, and they must stay in the room. Role play 'rooms' should always be safe spaces in person or online. Delegates are sometimes required to reveal parts of themselves which may make them feel incredibly vulnerable. They need to be able to do this in a psychologically safe, confidential and non-judgemental environment.

**'What happens in the room stays in the room.'**

Adhering to this is essential to your job as a role play actor.

On another note, as lovely as the role play world is, the role play companies compete for contracts and clients. So be conscious of what you say about one company or their work to another.

I would also be conscious of what you say when travelling to or from a job on public transport. I was once a role play actor on a highly confidential job centred around an unreleased product. I was on a train talking to another set of role players on a different job and accidentally mentioned the confidential job. On cue, another passenger jumped out of their seat and said, 'Are you talking about … My Dad invented that!' I was shocked, and needless to say, I learnt my lesson, never to do that again.

## Multi-Tasking

That unique skill that an actor has, to be in the moment on stage, committed to both character and story, while at the same time finding their light, riding audience laughter and obeying the blocking, is what you need to do during a role play. One part of your brain engages in the role play acting, while another part logs what has happened, enabling you to provide the participant with the all-important post role play feedback.

## Feedback

Actors live in a world of feedback, from the audition to the rehearsal room to the critics. The nature of our work requires us to receive constant feedback. This sensitivity to feedback will give you the building blocks to understand what is needed to provide brilliant, robust, unarguable feedback as a role play actor.

'After twenty years as a corporate roleplay writer and facilitator the actors that I love working with best have two qualities:

They have learnt their lines
They are on time

The other qualities that bring joy into my roleplay life are:

They have done the requested research
They muck in as a team
They speak up when there is unfair treatment'

Ali Hendry-Ballard
Inclusion Trainer and Consultant

# CHAPTER SEVEN

# It's not about you

I do have some bad news. This work is never about you. Corporate role play is not for all actors. If you cannot leave yourself alone and leave your ego at the door, it is unlikely that you will succeed as a corporate role play actor. Your 'performance' is there for the benefit and learning of the participant. You are a training tool and must always stick to the role play brief. You are responding to what that participant gives you in that moment. It is not your opportunity to see how emotional you can get, see how many times you can cry, show them how funny you are, or if you can channel the character needed for tomorrow's audition. It is not your chance to impress the delegate with your acting skills. You will undoubtedly do this anyway if you are truthful to the moment and the brief.

'An acting job is all about you. The stage is your platform. The spotlight is on you.

A role play job is NOT about you. It is all about the candidate/delegate. The spotlight is on them. The floor is their stage. It is all about their performance.'

Amanda Band
Managing Director – SimPatiCo UK Ltd

Role play is undoubtedly a chance to flex your acting muscles, and you are essentially improvising, but it must be within the parameters of the character and the brief.

It is essential to have the conversation with yourself and ensure you are entering this industry for the right reasons.

Like every industry, your reputation is what will get you re-employed. If a role play company feels you are not respecting the craft, your time within the industry will be short-lived. Role play companies put great trust in you when they send you out on a job, so they, and us at The Communication Practice, will often ask their current pool of role players for recommendations. You want to be the type of role player that is recommended time and time again. My golden rule on this front is to be friendly, professional, and easy to work with, and always remember that this work is never about you.

# CHAPTER EIGHT

# What is in it for you?

After twenty years in the business, I still find my work as a role play actor incredibly rewarding. Every job is unique, and I work alongside brilliant, talented people. Working as a role player is the best side hustle you can have as an actor. It provides considerable acting and life benefits.

I have benefited from all the points I make in this chapter. Don't get me wrong: it is not always plain sailing, and I will cover some of the challenges you may face working as a role play actor in my chapter: 'How to manage life as a role play actor,' but for now, let's focus on the positives.

## Acting benefits

It is better for you to be doing some form of acting in between acting gigs rather than doing any of the countless other jobs that resting actors often have to do; waiting tables, pulling pints, handing out leaflets, working in retail or at a reception desk. When role playing, you use your acting muscles and creative juices. Even if some types of role play work initially feel less creative, they still are. You use your imagination to create characters, an imaginary world, and a backstory. It means that creating these things, often very quickly, for an audition is more manageable. I have been in situations when the auditions were quiet, and I wasn't doing much role play work in between. When the audition email did come from my agent, I was, of course, excited but did feel a little rusty. This wasn't, and isn't, the case when I regularly work as a role play actor.

Role play is basically a form of improvisation. Improvisation is a fundamental part of acting. Being able to react, create, be in the moment, and build on what another actor has given you is a required skill in any rehearsal room. Role play work will continually enhance your improvisation skills. I remember panicking and stressing over a recall audition with the legendary improvisational film director Mike Leigh. While walking one day, I reminded myself that all Mike would be asking me to do is what I have done in boardrooms, offices and conference centres across the country. I just needed to improvise with him, as I had done with countless accountants, office managers and police officers. I didn't get that part, but I know I did the best I could on that day in that audition room. And coincidentally, Mike did call and offer me a different, smaller part in that same improvised film a year later.

As you move from one role play job to the next, you constantly work on new scripts and characters. Some role play scripts can be challenging to bring to life, as the client can sometimes write them and may focus too much on the technical elements of a job role rather than on the human characters within the role play scenarios. But this can present you with a great opportunity. If you can bring a script like that to life, you will fly when presented with a brilliantly written piece of drama.

In terms of character, what a privilege to explore so many in a sometimes very short space of time. Once in ten days, I played a twelve-year-old child, a marketing manager, a sergeant in the British Army, a law graduate and a chicken-shop customer.

Another thing I love about working as a role play actor is that I get to peep into industries and worlds that I previously knew nothing about. Much of my role play work has been with the British Army, a workforce I massively pre-judged before working with them. They are now one of my favourite organizations to work with. I remember finding it strange how comfortable I began to feel walking around army bases in an army uniform. The day a Major screamed at me for being on my mobile phone didn't even faze me. Once he had calmed down, I explained that I was a role play actor working there for the day. I then had to call my concerned grandmother, whom I had been on the phone with, and explain what had just happened.

Also, from an acting point of view, I get to observe and absorb the world. You may get an audition or be cast in an environment you have role played in many times. This will give you a massive head start, and casting directors love this sort of thing.

Screen work often requires you to reproduce the same performance repeatedly to accommodate all the different shooting angles. Some medical role play jobs may require you to present the same scenario five, ten or twenty times in one day. This is an excellent opportunity to practise reproducing the same character, opening gambit or energy for each medical exam candidate. Medical role play days can be pretty gruelling, so this a brilliant way to flip it and see it as training for your screen work.

The same goes for your emotional consistency. One of the challenges of acting on screen is the ability to reproduce full and genuine emotions repeatedly. This is especially true for me when my close-up is at the end of a long filming day. I continue to work on this screen job by screen job, but role play has been a valuable practising ground. Over the years, I have had to play some very emotionally charged role play characters, including neglected and abused children. Reproducing this emotion several times daily has proven helpful for my screen work.

Spending days with actors can be hugely beneficial when you are not working in traditional acting jobs. Being on the audition treadmill can be a very lonely place. When you can feel like you are the only one not getting jobs, auditions, recalls or any contact from your agent. Sharing these worries with other actors, over lunch, on a role play job can be incredibly empowering as you discover that you are not the only one feeling like this. I have also seen actors share practical advice and guidance in these moments. It can present an excellent opportunity to collaborate and share ideas. I know actors who met on role play jobs and then worked together on short films, podcasts and TV pilots.

Remember to lead with empathy when you are around other actors. If you are fortunate enough to book jobs and recalls, be sensitive with that information. I am not asking you to lie, just to be aware that it might be hard for some people to hear when they are not feeling great about their careers. Please read the room in this respect.

'I've always found that Corporate Role Play is a fantastic space for an actor to flex their acting muscles and challenge themselves as an artist. A safe space to create a character that will consistently be challenged and provoked. A space to explore how your character and yourself as an actor will respond to different people, challenges and scenarios. And a space where you are forced to create a nuanced and layered piece of work that is considered and intelligently crafted.

Corporate Role Play is a skill that I feel is invaluable and imperative in an actor's toolkit.'

Alim Jadavji
Actor

# Life benefits

Unless qualified in a particular area, you will generally earn more per hour working as a role play actor than doing most other actor side hustles.

Your pay rate as a role play actor can vary massively, depending on the role play company you are working for, the sector you are working in, whether you are required to provide feedback, and whether the job is virtual or in person. When starting out, you may be happy to accept a low fee to gain experience, but please be careful. When role playing, you use your acting talent and skill. A skill in which you have invested time, energy and, if you went to drama school, money; please do not allow yourself to be exploited. Navigating the sometimes-contradictory world of role player fees can be challenging, so I encourage you to always talk openly to other role players about fees for jobs.

I would say that the minimum you should be getting paid per day as a new role player is £150. For context, the current Equity minimum performer rate for subsidized theatre is £482 for a five-day week (£96.40 a day).

Your role play rate of pay can, of course, vary for the reasons I have stated, but within time that could be in the region of £300 or £400 mark per day if you move into the arena of becoming an actor facilitator.

You are usually paid for rehearsals separately, but some jobs may require you to attend briefing phone calls or virtual meetings as part of the fee. This can be especially true if it is a long-running job with many dates. This is often referred to as a rollout in the role play world.

Filmed role play should always pay you a higher fee, which will include your buyout, as they are also paying for future usage.

You know how much you need to earn per month to live. Making more per day or hour via role play will free up your time to do other valuable life activities, such as hobbies, reading, writing, developing another skill, seeing family and friends and looking after your mental health. These are all essential important life recreations that can become impossible when working fifty hours a week. Having more free time also means that when an audition does come in, you have the required time to prepare for it.

I also feel that, from a mental health perspective, it is vital to have a day or a weekend off of work. The acting industry requires a lot of commitment from us, but working seven days a week is not good for anybody's mental well-being.

One of the benefits of the COVID-19 pandemic and the subsequent worldwide lockdowns was the embracement of virtual working. This had a significant impact on the role play industry. Being able to role play virtually means you can now role play from anywhere in the world. You don't need to live in or travel to a major city. It also means you can squeeze a short role play job into a busy day or even multiple role play jobs into one day. I recently worked with London participants until 4 pm and then participants from New York from 5 pm to 10 pm. An example illustrating the superb opportunities working virtually now affords the global role play industry.

While I'm on the COVID-19 pandemic, referring to corporate role play as only a side hustle massively devalues the importance of the work, the skills it gives you and the revenue stream it can provide. In March 2020, I was performing in *La Cage aux Folles* at London's Park Theatre. Like many, I was unemployed overnight, with no immediate prospects of earning my living through acting. It was terrifying.

It was role play that saved the day. By May 2020, I was one of the first in the UK arm of the industry to take the work onto the virtual platform Zoom. This work supported me until I secured my first acting job at the end of 2020. I do not wish another pandemic on any of us. But it is a timely reminder that corporate role play is a valuable skill that will serve you incredibly well when there are no acting opportunities.

If you want to work from your living room, the role play industry can facilitate this. You can also use it as a way to see the world. As a role player, I have been to Geneva, Lisbon, Paris and Prague, to name a few places. When there, I was busy working, but I would generally have a few evenings free to see the city. I know some role players who have extended their trips to enable them to see the city before or after a role play job. Some have been fortunate enough to go to far-flung and exotic places and even fly business or first class.

A word of warning: I am very selective regarding role play work abroad. As you can imagine, sometimes you must cancel a role play job due to an acting audition or job. It is much more complicated to withdraw from a job when plane flights, foreign hotels and visas are involved.

When I accept a job abroad, I try not to do it too far in advance, and I prefer locations nearer to the UK. This is my preference to enable me to manage my acting and role play careers. Remember that some of your role play colleagues will no longer work as actors, so this will not be a worry for them. I am flagging it for you to keep at the back of your mind, as an offer of well-paid work in a glamorous location can be very attractive.

At the end of a day's work, there is no better feeling than feeling like you made a difference in somebody's life. This work can transform people's communication skills and lives. You may challenge them in a role play or provide a golden piece of feedback that could unlock their power and potential in the workplace. Not only in the workplace, but participants will hopefully also deploy these skills in their day-to-day interactions. I have bumped into delegates weeks, months and years after, who shared how much their communication skills developed after our work together.

# PART TWO

# HOW TO GET THE WORK AND KEEP ON WORKING

# CHAPTER NINE

# The research

The first step to working as a role play actor is to be taken on by one or a few role play companies. As I said, most, if not all, of your role play work will be you gaining jobs via a role play company instead of working directly for the client.

This may sound like an obvious answer, but Google is the best place to start your research. All role play companies must advertise their services via a website to enable their clients to find them. As with the companies, their websites will vary in scale and size, but their website should provide you with a clear indication of the type of role play work the company may be able to offer you. More importantly, it will let you know if you are currently the right actor for them at that time. More on this later.

When googling, I would use all of the following search terms to ensure you discover all of the role play companies that are out there:

Role play companies
Role play actor jobs
Medical role play jobs
Role play agency
Corporate role play jobs
Business role play
Drama-based training companies
Drama-based corporate training

Whenever I google the above, I notice a new company I haven't seen before, so it is worth doing this regularly. Maybe set a reminder to do it monthly. If a new company does launch, and you are one of the first actors to contact them, it could put you in a prime position to gain an audition with them.

I am sure you have several friends who have corporate jobs. Whether in finance, education, government, retail, pharmaceutical or the military. It is worth probing those closest to you to find out if their job role requires them to have any contact with role play companies that they could put you in touch with.

You may have a friend who works in Human Resources (HR), Learning and Development (L&D) or Equity, Diversity and Inclusion (EDI). These departments are the most likely to engage with role play companies for their company's communication training needs. Your friend could be a role play companies' client and therefore could connect you with that role play company.

Also, please speak to your family and friends about their experience with role play at work. I am sure that they will have thoughts and opinions on this subject. They may also have recently completed some training that used role play and role play actors. They may know the name of the role play company; this is a great and powerful way to introduce yourself to that role play company. For example:

> Dear Role Play Company,
>
> My name is Syrus Lowe, and I am very interested in joining your pool of role play actors. I have just been on your website and am very drawn to the type of work you are doing. My cousin, Jane Lowe, participated in a training course you ran recently at Mastercard. She said she thought the Crucial Conversations role play session was incredibly powerful, the best training she had ever had, and that the actors were fantastic. My role play experience is…
> Kind regards,
> Syrus Lowe

If you went to a drama school, it is worth contacting that network to enquire about role play opportunities. I am sure that some of your contemporaries will be working as role play actors. Having trained with you, they can vouch for your skill and professionalism.

So much of the ability to gain role play work is via recommendation. Many of my drama school contemporaries do role play work; I have worked on role play jobs with five different people I trained at drama school with. You never know; one of your peers may be running their own role play or communication training company.

It is also worth reaching out to your drama school and seeing if the school or teachers have any role play links or contacts.

The same goes for your friends who are professional actors. They may currently be or have previously worked for a role play company, even just completed an acting job with, or be friends with, someone who runs a role play company.

Once you start working as a role player, your new role player friends are an excellent resource for information about role play work. They may currently work for a company that is looking for an actor like you, are aware of a company that is starting up or an existing company that has just secured a large amount of work. The role play world is one in which people share their contacts. As I have said, role play companies appreciate it when people come to them via a recommendation. It is important to remember this from the day of your first role play job. You could be working alongside someone who could secure you future employment. Yet another reason for you to be at your best and most professional on every role play job you are on.

My company, The Communication Practice, secured a large piece of work in 2022. We had to pitch for this work, but I now know that the client was initially interested in working with us because they had, themselves, role played opposite me a few years before.

Social media, especially LinkedIn, is a great way to see what role play companies exist. You don't require a LinkedIn profile as an actor, but as a role player, it can be a great way to connect with role play companies and get on their radars. Once you start working as a role player, it is worth following any of the clients you work with. Seeing the client's public posts is a great way to get an insight into their culture and people. Following the client doesn't need to be restricted to LinkedIn; Twitter, Facebook and Instagram are great platforms for gaining more insights.

You will be surprised at which conversations or encounters can lead to you getting role play work. Once you start talking about this subject, it can be amazing what contacts connected to the industry you may already have within your networks. I have gained a fair amount of role play work from conversations I have struck up in the most random settings; weddings, theatre opening nights, family gatherings, holidays and yoga classes. As I said earlier, most people have a connection, opinion or story on role play, so it can often come up in conversation.

'Edinburgh festival, 2004. By day, suited and booted as a role-player for a big pharmaceutical company. By night, on stage in my costume performing in a play. I felt like a double-agent and couldn't believe my luck. Any of you who have performed at the festival know how expensive it is to take part, those role player fees certainly helped ease my financial pain that year.

I soon discovered that I felt more fulfilled in a training room than on stage and shifted my focus to pursuing a career in the world of corporate role playing. I was receiving far more praise and recognition from colleagues, clients and participants than I ever did from casting directors and agents. Many of my friends still perform, some have stopped altogether. Most of them manage a dual career though, the thrill of the double agent. Sometimes actor, sometimes role player ...'

Justin McCarron
Director of Programmes – Edison Red Ltd

# CHAPTER TEN

# Role play company websites

When you land on a role play companies' website, investigate the whole site and the type of work they do.

It should be clear on most of the role play company's websites how they want you to contact them. Some will have dedicated actor submission email addresses or a web form page on their site.

Whichever way they ask you to contact them, follow it. You will get off to a bad start if you annoy them at the outset by not following their particular procedure.

The other important thing to mention is that their website may contain the following type of statement:

Our books are full; therefore, we are not currently accepting any actor submissions.

If it does say something like this, please <u>DO NOT</u> contact them, not even if you think you are the perfect actor for them. Just note their website and put a reminder in your diary to revisit it in a few months.

If they are accepting actor submissions, make sure you submit what they have asked for, as different companies require different things. It is worth making a note of what each company asks of you.

If they ask you to email them using a specific 'Email subject heading,' please do use it. Also, do not send large photo or video attachments. They may get automatically deleted as they may risk clogging up the company's inbox.

I feel I have become a bit bossy in this chapter, but it is all to give you the best possible opportunities with the role play companies. Mistakes are easy to make when you are enthusiastic and sending lots of emails. As I said in the introduction, a lot of this advice comes off the back of mistakes that I have made in the past.

There are some things that most companies will ask you for. These include:

A cover letter/email telling them about you and your experience.
Whether you have attended a course at an accredited drama school.
A link to your Spotlight page.
A link to your showreel, if it is not on your Spotlight page.

They may ask you to keep an eye on their social media postings for upcoming opportunities. Most role play companies don't have huge social media followings, so following them on all of theirs, liking and retweeting their content, may help get you onto their radar.

Some other things worth mentioning are that some will advertise their pool of actors on their site, and others won't. There is no rhyme or reason to this, but if they do, it will give you a sense of which actors they already have and if there are any casting gaps that you can fill.

The companies will also vary massively regarding the number of actors on their books. Most companies work on the assumption that a percentage of their actors will be unavailable for periods due to theatre and filming work, so they will account for that in terms of the total number of actors they have.

Some companies refer to their actors as role players, some as associates, and some just use the term actors.

There are a minority of companies that do not state on their website how they want you to contact them. These tend to be newer companies that, luckily, find themselves very busy from the outset and have yet to develop their entire websites. In this case, email them regarding your interest in working with them, or give them a phone call. I did this exact thing with one company. I called them, and they said they were not currently recruiting actors. We then chatted about my work and life experience, and it turned out that I used to live on the same road their office was on. Before they signed off the call, they told me to send my stuff across and that they would take a look. I auditioned for them a few months later, and they eventually became one of my primary role play employers for many years.

When investigating a role play company's website, please pay close attention to the industries and clients they advertise as working with. It would be best if you made sure that these industries and companies potentially being your end client is something you are comfortable with on an ethical basis. I know some role players who have made it clear to a role play company that they are unwilling to work with the tobacco, oil and gas, pharmaceutical or nuclear industries. Most role companies will understand this and should tell you during your audition if the majority of their work is in one of these sectors.

Like every other industry worldwide, the role play industry is trying to level the playing field regarding diversity and representation. It has historically been a very white, middle-class, university-educated industry. I have been on role play jobs where I have frankly been embarrassed that we role players have not reflected the diversity of the clients we are role playing for. All the role play companies know this area needs to change; a few have even personally involved me to assist with this change. This covers all aspects of diversity, including age, disability status, race, gender, sexual orientation or whether someone is neurodiverse.

This new thinking also applies to the archaic idea of needing to attend a particular type of drama school. This is very much a thing of the past. Demonstrating your acting skill via the credits on your CV or a showreel will get you through the doors of most role play companies. The role play industry needs to strive to represent the beautiful and diverse workforces it works with. I believe that the role play companies who fail to do this are the ones that will be left behind.

Humour is a great tool for practice scenarios if used gently, judiciously, and skilfully.

A shared observation laced with a twinkle in the eye, eases the intensity of a practice conversation and helps to build trust.

I remember playing a delegate's boss opposite him. Ten seconds into the exercise I stopped and said:

"You don't like me, do you?"
I was speaking in character but not in role.

The delegate laughed, then recovered and said:

"I think I know what the problem is. We have a dysfunctional relationship."
The penny had dropped, voice and posture changed.
Boom!'

Neil Bett
Frank Partners LLP

# CHAPTER ELEVEN

# The cover letter

The cover letter or email is the role play company's introduction to you. It is your first chance to show them your passion and professionalism.

Of course, you have standard email best practices to consider; a clear subject line, double check the email address is correct, triple-check the spelling of names, and proofread, proofread, proofread. This might all sound obvious, but it is easy to make small mistakes when sending dozens of emails quickly. I would send a few of the emails and then take a break. Or draft them all, leave it for a few hours, and give them a final check before sending.

For your cover email to grab the role play company's attention, I would ensure that you include all of the following:

Start with an introduction, and let them know that you want to work specifically with them, become one of their role players and join their team.

If you have trained at a drama school or another institution, tell them the name and when you graduated. A tiny handful of role play companies will only accept submissions from actors who have trained at accredited drama schools, but I would say that these are in the minority these days.

I would then provide a brief insight into your acting career. A few of your recent credits from different sections of the industry. Remember that they will have access to your Spotlight CV, so you don't need to go into too much detail here. Many role play companies are committed to employing role players who still work as actors, as they value the skills these actors bring from their work on stage, screen, in audio or gaming.

Next, you share your role play experience. Please be very honest about this. Tell them if you have lots of experience, but it is fine if you only have a few role play jobs under your belt or none at all. All role play companies understand that every role player must start somewhere. If you are the right casting for a job, and it is clear that you are, or have been, a professional actor, the role play company may take a chance and give you a break. If this is the case, they will provide you with opportunities to train and observe, ensuring you are ready for your first gig with them.

The role play company may reply to you saying that they would love for you to contact them again in the future when you have a bit more experience. If they say this, then do. They are not being polite. If they have said this, they have seen some promise in what you have shared with them in your cover email, CV and showreel.

This section of your cover email should also detail the types of role play you have done and whether you have delivered feedback to participants.

I would only mention the industries you have role played in and the clients you have role played for. I would not include the name of the role play companies you work for. You never know the professional or personal histories between role play companies or if a particular company's client previously worked with another role play company. If you meet with the role play company and they ask who else you work for, or have worked for in the past, then tell them, but you don't need to mention it in your initial cover email. This is not the case if you were, in fact, recommended to write to them by another role play company.

*I believe that this is the most important part of your cover email:*

**Your real-world work experience.** Clients are always encouraged when they feel that a role play actor has experience in their particular industry. They think it means you understand how their industry works, the terminology, some of the acronyms, and, more importantly, the industry's communication challenges. Experience in law, accounting, financial services, the military and many other industries will all stand you in good stead.

Say your side hustle was working as a weekend manager in a pub for many years. Then the role play company you work for secures a large amount of role play work from a large pub chain to improve their staff's customer service skills; you will be in prime position to be a part of the role player team.

Do spend a reasonable amount of time thinking about and listing all your jobs from over the years. There may be some that you would rather forget, but they could be the ones that unlock and begin your role play career with a particular role play company.

Share with them the industry, the company, and your role. Mention if the job required you to use your communication or feedback skills. If you have a long list of previous employers, this might be better detailed on your non-acting CV, but you can still give them a flavour of this in your cover email.

If you know any of their current actors, mention it, and also let the actors know that you have written to the role play company. So much of securing this work, and a spot within a role play company, is via recommendation. If one of their trusted actors gives you the thumbs up, that will get you off to a fine start with the company.

Do list any other languages you speak. You must speak this language to an incredibly high standard as you will need to be able to role play and, potentially, give feedback to participants in this language. This is another important one, as a lot of the role play companies now work with clients with a global workforce. For many, the standard company-wide language spoken will be English, but it is always a bonus when they can offer employees the chance to role play in their native tongue.

Try to reference some of their work or clients in your email. If they specialize in a particular sector or type of role play, then mention that. You want the company to feel like you have taken the time to investigate their work, client base and website.

In the world of role play, playing age is a broad thing. I know actors in their fifties who are incredibly convincing when role playing as a child. The role play company will clearly understand your age from your headshot. You don't need to mention this in your cover email, as it will be on your spotlight page.

It is probably worth attaching your current headshot to the email. It will be on your Spotlight page, but I think it's nice to have it attached. It will probably open up when they click on the email and might immediately spark their interest.

Send a high-resolution file, but do not send one too big as this may result in the email may getting deleted before they look at it.

If you have a selection of headshots, choose the one where you look most professional in a corporate sense. Imagine you work for a corporate company and are selecting a photo for your ID badge. Choose the headshot that is closest to this. If you only have one headshot, don't worry. Please do not feel the need to spend money on a corporate headshot session.

Your showreel will be on your Spotlight page. It is not necessary to attach or share a link to it; you can mention in your email that it is contained within your spotlight page.

Spotlight now allows you to list several skills that cover the role play part of the performance industry. If you are skilled in any of the following areas, then do make sure you include it on your Spotlight page:

<u>Other Skills Section</u>
Drama workshop leader
Improvisation
Soft Skills Trainer (*soft skills are communication skills*)
Corporate Role Play

<u>Performance</u>
Autocue trained/experienced
Role Play
Forum Theatre

<u>Presenting Section</u>
Conference Presenting
Corporate

My final word on Spotlight is to keep your skills and credits up to date. As you know, or will soon discover, the acting industry is tiny. You may have worked with the best friend of a role play company owner; the owner may have recently seen you on stage or screen. Seeing your acting brilliance, no matter how brief, may jog their memory and encourage them to invite you for a chat or audition.

If you are not currently on Spotlight, that is fine. It is not a pre-requisite to becoming a role play actor. You may be taking a break from acting or are no longer acting in the traditional sense. If that is the case, make that clear to the role play company and ensure that you attach a headshot, CV, and possibly a link to a previous showreel, to your cover email.

Do let them know if you have a driving licence. Some role play jobs may require a member of the acting team to drive the set, equipment or other team members.

Finally, let them know if you have accommodation in other cities. When I say accommodation, I mean a close family member or friend with a spare room or sofa or who works away a lot themselves. Nine times out of ten, when an overnight stay is required, the client will be willing to pay for a hotel for the role player team. There are those odd occasions when the budgets are incredibly tight, and having this secondary accommodation may be the thing that swings the job your way.

# CHAPTER TWELVE

# Organizational skills

As hinted in the last chapter, you may send dozens of emails to dozens of role play companies, with as many follow-up or reminder emails. It can be challenging to keep track of all of this, especially if these interactions occur over months or even years, and if the personnel at a role play company changes during this time.

Persistence and fantastic organizational skills are vital to enter this industry. Once you enter it and start working for a few companies, the organizational skills you need are considerable, from managing your diary to ensuring you have all of the relevant role player material in a timely fashion to invoicing the role play company correctly.

Being organized when sending these initial cover emails will be great practice for the skills you will need throughout your role play career.

I have always used spreadsheets for managing this type of data. One of my side hustles for many years was as a receptionist, so I am well acquainted with spreadsheets. I currently use Microsoft Excel or the Apple program Numbers, depending on the project. You have to purchase these products, but several free spreadsheet products exist. If spreadsheets aren't for you, use the notes section on your phone, a notebook or your diary. Whatever works best for you; make sure that it is a system that makes sense and will continue to make sense if you need to refer back to it years later.

# CHAPTER THIRTEEN

# The audition

Role play companies do not hold auditions very often, so if invited to attend one, I would do everything possible to get there. Generally, a role play company may not hold auditions more than once or twice a year or only hold them when they need to increase their pool of role play actors. They like to remain loyal to their current pool by being able to offer each actor a reasonable amount of work per year. This is another reason some companies may go some time without substantially increasing their pool of actors. Also, delivering role play work and trying to source new clients often consumes role play companies' time, so auditioning new role players can fall off their priority list.

The audition may be in person or virtual. It may be just an introductory chat or start with this and then involve you practising a role play.

The role play company will want to get to know you and your personality. To explore if they feel they can and want to work with you and ultimately trust you to represent their company, brand and values. You will go out in small teams or on your own on some jobs, so this trust is vital.

As with the cover email, you want the role play company to feel that you want to work specifically for them, so do your research before the audition. Exhaust their website, do a Google search on them to source any other information, and research the people who run the company, specifically those you are meeting. LinkedIn is an excellent resource; most role play companies now use it to promote their work and share relevant articles or new research in their field.

> "It's not like that in the real world," says anyone who ever wants to get out of a "role play" situation. And that's why using professional actors during learning events is a game-changer: it gets around the awkwardness of "practising" with your colleagues. As well as being a convincing "colleague," I make sure people I work with are skilled at giving considered feedback and are prepared to do their homework before turning up at a client.'
>
> Carrie Stockton
> Odyssey People Development

The audition chat is also an opportunity to find out if they are a company you want to work for. Make sure you ask all of your questions and be in a place of curiosity. Those you are meeting should share with you the make-up of the company and the type of work they do. They should also be transparent about how much they pay, how many days they take to pay, and how much work their actors generally get from them. Most people who now run role play companies were once freelance role players, so they understand the importance of knowing these things. If they don't mention them, please ask at the end of the conversation. It is vital that you leave with this information. Also, it is okay if you decide they are not the right company for you. You have to trust your gut on this. In the past, I have said no to certain role play companies as something about their energy was off. I probably couldn't describe exactly what it was, but I knew something about them wasn't right for me. As Granny would say, 'My spirit didn't take to them.'

As I said, this chat or audition could occur on a virtual platform. If it does, then all of the above still applies, but you should bear a few extra things in mind. We all know that virtual communication can be more of a challenge as you are not in the same room as the person you are talking to. However, there are some simple tips and tricks that can make the conversation feel more natural and therefore enable you to be more impactful.

When talking, try to look directly into your webcam. The instinct will be for you to look at their face on the screen when you speak, but from their perspective, it won't feel like you are looking directly at them. My rule of thumb is to look into the webcam when you are talking and look at their face on the screen when you are listening to them. Try to bounce between the two during the conversation. **This is a great thing to start practising from now on when you find yourself communicating on a virtual platform.**

Best practice is to have your source of light behind your computer facing you, whether that is a natural or artificial light source. If the light source is behind you, it will create a shadow, and they won't be able to see you very well.

You want your webcam to be in line with your eyes, so you can sit up straight and look directly into the webcam. To be clear, you don't achieve this by tilting the screen up or down but by raising the height of your laptop. There are more technical and costly ways to accomplish this, but I place my laptop on top of a few large books. You could even stand during the conversation if you have a standing desk or a few more books. I do this often on virtual calls when I am tired, as it gives me an energy boost. The person on the other end of the call will have no idea if you are standing or sitting, so it won't make any difference to them.

From their perspective, you want to take up as much of the screen as possible. Think of the framing of a television newsreader. There is a small gap above their head and to their sides, but their face and torso take up most of the frame. This ensures that the person you are talking to focuses solely on you and not the other things in your environment.

All these things will indicate that you are comfortable working and communicating on a virtual platform, which is incredibly important, as I imagine that a percentage of the work you are offered by a role play company will be virtual.

Virtual or in person, if they ask you to practise a role play scenario, they will have sent this to you in advance. It will be a role play that is typical of their type of work. If this is the case, review what I share in the 'How to do corporate role play' chapter and apply those skills to the scenario they have sent you.

The level of preparation you give to this audition scenario will indicate to the company how well prepared you will be ahead of a job.

In an audition setting, you would 'play' the role play actor, and the person auditioning you would 'play' the participant. So, you would effectively be playing the role you would do on an actual role play job.

They may ask you to give them some feedback after the role play. That would be you as the role play actor providing feedback to the person auditioning you as if they were a participant. Role play companies understand that actors are often in very different places when it comes to being able to deliver feedback. Feedback is a skill that develops over time, job after job. All you can do in an audition is try your best; the company will know that this will improve over time and that you may be nervous in an audition setting.

At the end of the audition, they may provide you with feedback on your role play and feedback skills. This a golden opportunity to get some feedback from an industry expert. There is also every chance they won't provide you any in-the-moment feedback. This is in no way an indication of how well you have done. If it is a team auditioning you, they will likely want to have a discussion internally before providing you with any feedback.

After the audition, the role play company will always email you letting you know the outcome. If they haven't given you any feedback, I would use this opportunity to ask for some. It should indicate which areas of role play and/or feedback you should focus on developing.

The audition may be a full day or half day if it is in person. This was the more typical way of holding auditions before the COVID-19 pandemic. The day would generally start with the company introducing themselves and then see each auditionee practising a role play scenario. Typically, they won't pay you to attend these audition days. However, they do usually provide lunch and may pay for your travel.

As daunting as auditioning in front of other auditionees may be, it is a great chance to watch and learn. There will be a range of experiences in the room, and it will be good to see how different actors respond to, sometimes the same, role play material. It is also another opportunity to start growing your role play network. If you strike up a friendship with another auditionee, they may become a helpful source of information, contact or become someone you can even practise role playing with.

After the audition, I would share with the role play company that you thoroughly enjoyed the day and are happy to observe some of their upcoming deliveries to get a feel for their work. It is unlikely that the role play company will pay you for this observation, but it does show a great deal of enthusiasm and thirst for the work on your part. I feel that you don't need to do this with any company on more than two occasions.

'As an employer, we look for people with the dual ability to both act and coach. People who can portray a character flexibly and authentically in a semi-scripted or improvised performance and who understand the goals and context of corporate learning and development. People who serve the needs of the individual or group, and who are able to explore difficult territory, if that's what's required. People who can simultaneously monitor and remember what the participant is doing and how their character is feeling, so they can then give effective feedback with courage, integrity and compassion.'

Antony Quinn
Co-Founder, The Communication Practice

# CHAPTER FOURTEEN

# What to do ahead of your first role play job

Being offered your first job by a role play company is a considerable achievement and a testament to all the hard work you put in beforehand. Congratulations, if this is the case. Hopefully, it will be the first of many and the beginning of a lengthy professional relationship. You want to start as you mean to go on and give them a clear indication of your professionalism from the get-go.

Role play companies are generally busy and may be trying to source dozens of actors for a particular job. Respond as quickly as you can to all of their emails and messages. You will get in their good books immediately by being the person who always responds straight away. I often get thanked by role play companies for my 'speedy response', which does make me wonder how long other role play actors are making them wait.

They may fill some jobs on a first-come, first-served basis; in this case, it is in your best interest to reply as quickly as possible.

As you build the relationship, I encourage you always to personalize your emails by using their names. In the past, I have gone years before meeting my administrative contact at some role play companies, so the level of rapport we managed to build up over email was hugely important. I recently stopped working for one role play company; in her final email, the administration manager said she had '*really enjoyed our exchanges over the years*' – we only ever met in person once during our three-year working relationship.

Ahead of your first job, the role play company will send you several emails containing details about the job. I would get into the habit of always acknowledging that you have received their emails. It could be as simple as saying, 'Received with thanks.' Regarding the environmental impact, please don't feel you have to reply to every email they send you, just the ones containing essential information and if they specifically ask you to reply. Remember to hit 'reply' only to them and not 'reply all' when you do respond. The rest of the team of role players do not need to receive your 'Received with thanks' or 'Have a lovely weekend' courtesy email reply.

When you receive the role play brief or any other information relating to the job, read it at your earliest convenience. If anything needs to be clarified, then do ask. The role play company would prefer you ask them a dozen questions rather than go into a job unprepared. Once again, you are displaying your attention to detail. Doing this as early as possible is essential for allowing yourself time to digest all the material thoroughly.

I will share an example of the type of email you may receive before your first job in the next chapter.

Ensure you are aware of the required dress code before the job. What you wear can hugely impact how confident you feel walking into a corporate environment. It can vary; you don't want to be overdressed or underdressed on a role play job.

In my experience, the role play industry generally uses the following terms to define what style of dress they require on a job:

| | |
|---|---|
| Business Smart | Suit, tie, long sleeved shirt, conservative skirt, closed toe shoes, dark and neutral colours. |
| Business Casual | Shirt and sweatshirt, no tie, short-sleeved tops, open-toe shoes, polo shirt, bright colours. |
| Casual | Trainers, jeans, t-shirts, no formal dress code, dress to feel comfortable. |

It is within the realms of possibility that you may still need clarification on a particular job's dress code after reading this or when you have spoken to the role play company. If unsure, always err on the side of dressing smarter.

Ensure you research the client and the part of their business you are working with. Large companies, such as banks, can have many different divisions. There are usually very insightful short videos on their websites or YouTube that can get you up to speed on what a particular division does. Having some helpful jargon or terminology in your back pocket is incredibly helpful. Google the client to see if their business has been in the news lately. You want to arm yourself with as much background information as possible to feel confident and calm when playing that investment banker, social worker or civil servant.

Be clear on whom you are working alongside on the job. The role play company will send you all the names you need and possibly their phone numbers and email addresses. You can google most people now, and a picture of them will pop up, making it easier for you to find them at the start of the day.

The people you generally need to know are:

- The other role players
- The role play team leader
- The facilitator – if there is one on this particular job
- The client representative on the day
- Any representative from the role play company who will be there on the day (this is not a regular occurrence)

I always check the location of the job and the travel options ahead of the day. Some venues can be in remote places with limited transport options, and you may need to book a taxi before the day. Please don't assume, like I have before, that you can book an Uber when you arrive at the train station. Even if Uber does operate in the area, they may be few and far between. Some venues can also be hard to find as they are in large business complexes. Google Image is an excellent resource for seeing the venue and plotting your journey before the big day. You want to arrive calm, composed and ready to work. It might be an idea to call or email the venue to see if they have any tips or tricks for finding them.

There may be a virtual briefing call ahead of the job. This will certainly happen if the job is new or you are new to a long-running job. It will allow you to obtain all the relevant information and to ask questions. This may also be when you meet the other team members. Remember to use the virtual tips and tricks I shared in the last chapter. The role play company probably now delivers a lot of their work virtually, and this is an excellent chance for them to see that you are confident and competent when communicating on a virtual platform.

The role play company should pay you for your time on a briefing call, or they may package it into the overall fee for the job. I am finding that companies are generally paying £50 – £100 per hour for virtual briefings.

If it is a rollout job, the briefing call may be considered part of your unpaid pre-work. If the role play is straightforward, someone from the company may just want to check in with you via phone to ensure that you are happy with everything ahead of the job. This would not be paid but is a good indicator of the level of care and attention that particular role play company provides. This would be a great sign of a company I would like to work for.

'Time and experience enable you to have a calmer approach to receiving detailed briefs and not getting overwhelmed. Ensure you understand the context and your role on a high level. Remember you do not need to be an expert in the job you're portraying. Focus on the behavioural challenge you need to present for the participant. Having a crib sheet in whatever form works for your learning style is very helpful. I find the process of creating that crib sheet helps me absorb the information and gain clarity on the role and purpose of the interaction.'

Claire Lichie
Actor and Facilitator

# CHAPTER FIFTEEN

# What to do on your first role play job

Your first role play job or job for a new company is bound to be daunting. You may feel immense pressure and that you have to be perfect. Remember that you are learning and are, potentially, at the beginning of your journey. I am still learning twenty years after my first role play job; I always remind myself that every day is a school day.

As mentioned in the last chapter, you will always receive a job information email ahead of the day. Here is what one may look like:

Dear Syrus,

I hope this finds you well.

Thank you so much for agreeing to be one of the team of actors for the upcoming future leader's programme with Deloitte. We are assisting Deloitte with this program in which they equip the next generation of leaders with the tools they need for the future.

The programme runs for four days. We are joining on day four. The delegates will have explored a range of leadership tools and ideas. Day four is a chance for them to put these into action. All the delegates will participate in a role play with one of our role players.

There will be four role players, and you will do your role play five times with five different Deloitte future leaders throughout the day.

***You are doing <u>Role Play 3</u> – playing the role of Al Jenkins.***

*Tara Montgomery is the lead role player on the day, and her number is 07656345123.*

*Tara has worked on this programme for several years and knows the client and briefs very well.*

### *<u>Date</u>*

*Friday 16th August 2024*

### *<u>Timings</u>*

*08.30 arrival*
*09.30 Role play sessions start*
*15.30 Finish time*

### *<u>Location</u>*

*Bridge Room*
*Hilton Hotel*
*Reading*
*RG1 1AF*

*The nearest train station to the venue is Reading. Please get a taxi from here.*

### *<u>Fee</u>*

*£285 + travel costs*

*Please send all receipts with your invoice*

*Please send your invoice within 72 hours of the job.*

*I have attached your role play brief, the delegate brief, and more information on the programme.*

*Please reply to let me know that you have received this email.*

*Kind regards,*

*Drama-Training Worldwide*

It is in the role play company's best interest to ensure you are fully prepared for your first job. If a role player team leader or facilitator is on the job, the role play company will likely introduce you to them ahead of the day. You may even have the opportunity to travel with them to the job, a brilliant chance to build rapport, gain some extra insights and ask any questions you may have. Sometimes there are details and quirks about a particular job that the role play company may not be aware of, but the facilitator or team leader is.

As soon as you arrive at the venue, consider yourself as 'on'. Whether engaging with the building's security team, the receptionist or the client, you represent and are an ambassador of the role play company. Be aware of what you are projecting the whole time. You are not in the relaxed environment of a rehearsal room full of actors. I have failed in this area in the past. I am a laid-back, casual person with quite a loud laugh, and I have sometimes forgotten where I am and, in the past, have needed a gentle reminder from those I am working with that I am in a corporate setting.

The role play company will likely ask one of your role player colleagues how you were on this first job for them. Not only asking about your role play work but also your professionalism throughout the day. As a role player, you live in a world of feedback that starts from day one.

Role play days vary in length. Some require you to travel on the day, and some will need you to stay over the night before.

Your first job is an excellent opportunity to be at your most curious, to watch everyone at work and see how they conduct themselves throughout the day. Of course, you may get to observe an experienced role player role playing. But you will also see how your fellow role players interact with each other, the delegates, the client and how they navigate a corporate environment. It is also a chance for you to see the behaviour of the delegates, as the character you are playing may have a similar personality to one or even some of them. The venue may be a dedicated training venue or hotel, but it may also be the delegate's work environment. This is a golden opportunity to watch them in their natural habitat and to pick up any business jargon and behaviours that may be useful to you during this and future jobs.

'I can remember my first role playing experience and being terrified that I would be discovered for knowing nothing about what I was talking about. Apart from the fact that this was true, the important point was I wasn't there to be an expert in finance and accounting, but in behaviour. Now I'm involved in running a business myself, I've come to realise that everyone is working it out as they go along. You can give them something they can't get anywhere else. And if you are scared on your first time, don't worry, Sally from the marketing team will be twice as scared as you are!'

Charlie Walker-Wise
RADA Business

The role play company should have informed you of their expenses policy before the job. Most clients will pay, via the role play company, for your travel expenses, and lunch if it is all full day. I would take pictures of all travel and lunch receipts on the day, so you can find them quickly when submitting your invoice. Some role play companies will require you to send these receipts, and others won't. You can attach the images to your invoice email if they need them.

Most companies will expect you to book and pay for your travel and then invoice them for it, along with your fee for the job. The company may book it for you if it is an expensive train or flight fare.

Regarding booking hotels, that is generally more varied and again will depend on the price. The company may prefer to book the rooms themselves as they can sometimes get a bulk discount for booking several rooms.

If you are not in the financial position to pay for any of these things, please let the role play company know. They will understand that not all actors can pay for their expenses upfront and be reimbursed by the company thirty days later.

Some companies are also happy for you to pay for these things and then pay you back straight away.

Some companies may ask you to share taxis with your role player colleagues to save on costs.

Please ensure you know the pay for your day's work. I have been on role play jobs where role players have asked me, a fellow role player, what their pay is and what expenses they can claim back. Very few people do a day's work, not knowing how much they are paid. If the company haven't told you, it is probably an admin oversight rather than for any immoral reason. I have realized over the years that because those who work at role play companies are employed and on set yearly salaries, they can easily forget how important it is for us self-employed role players to know exactly what we are being paid for each day's work, as our income can vary dramatically from month to month.

It is unlikely that the role play company will have told the client that this is your first role play job; I encourage you not to share this information. Clients can get nervous about new role players, and having this information may create unnecessary anxiety.

To grow as a role player, you need constant feedback on your role playing and feedback skills. You will continually develop and learn and should embrace receiving guidance and advice from your role play seniors. You should start this process after your first job. Ask your team leader, fellow role player or facilitator if they have any feedback for you. An excellent way to frame it is to ask if they feel there is anything you could have done differently. They should be used to delivering developmental feedback, so they should deliver it with care. I am sure they will also share many things you did brilliantly.

Along with the positive and developmental feedback you have received, I would make a note of useful things that will assist you the next time you are on a role play job for that client or in that venue: the name of the client, any useful business jargon for that sector of the clients business, the phone numbers of the local taxi services and any particular travel or logistical quirks. I would get in the habit of doing this for every job. Sometimes you can return to a client or venue years later, and these notes will prove incredibly helpful and again highlight, to your colleagues, your attention to detail.

After your first job, I would also email the role play company, letting them know you thoroughly enjoyed the work and meeting the team. Also, let them know that you are around and available for any upcoming work and that you would love to hear if there is any feedback for you to help you grow as a role player. This last feedback question is worth asking, as the client or one of the delegates may have provided some to the role play company after the event. A positive piece of feedback from a client or delegate, no matter how brief, will stand you in excellent stead with a new role play company.

'It was my first ever corporate role play job in Stafford. All I had been sent prior was a video of the simulation that the delegates would be going through. I thought, "Oh, this is easy. Nothing to learn!" I arrived to meet my fellow role player and the first thing she asked was, "So how did you get on with the scenarios?" I replied, "What scenarios?!" To cut the long story short, I was not sent the email with said scenarios. However, I told myself to stay in the moment, be a sponge and remember I was there to assist the learning of the delegates. I was not on trial. This enabled me to relax and remember all the key bits of information I needed throughout the day. This is the same mentality I have carried with me throughout my whole experience in recent years, and I would say are key tips to being an effective corporate role player and facilitator.'

Abraham Tiyamiyu
Actor Facilitator

# CHAPTER SIXTEEN

# Steal with pride

I have a confession to make. Everything I have shared with you so far in this book I have stolen from someone else. Not all from the same person but hundreds of role players, facilitators and participants I have worked with over the years. I have no bad feelings about this as I know that they, in turn, stole it from someone else. That is the beauty of this sort of work. The more you do it, the more intuitive it becomes, and the more little nuggets you can pick up from the people you work with. The level of observation and curiosity I encouraged you to have on your first job should be with you on every job. There are always new skills and approaches to steal – sorry, learn.

'One of the things I love about learning and development work is that you are also constantly learning. It requires the ability to listen carefully, and step outside of your own needs and wants - your own personal agenda. Not only is that a useful skill to practise as an actor and as a human being, but when you're in the learning and development room working with other facilitators, there's a lot of useful knowledge that one can absorb. It's an opportunity to use all the skills of an actor - our observation of human behaviours - in a powerful, unique and beneficial way. Being there for others, not yourself, is incredibly satisfying. It's a service and a privilege.'

Martin Delaney
Actor and Coach

When I work as a facilitator, I encourage participants to steal the good behaviours they see demonstrated by their colleagues, and you should do the same. Whether you have a physical notebook or do it on your phone, it is worth having a little area to store all your golden nuggets and tips. If you are anything like me, it is also worth using this space to jot down names, technical jargon or business acronyms, anything that can help you in the long run or when working with that client or sector again. This kind of attention to detail will assist you in appearing professional, proactive and observant. And you never know; one day, someone may be stealing little nuggets from you.

# CHAPTER SEVENTEEN

# How to manage your life as a role play actor

One of the critical components to a lifelong side hustle as a corporate role play actor is an incredibly high level of organization. You are managing your role play career alongside your acting career. There will be clashes and times when you must make difficult decisions, but all you can do is try your best to mitigate them.

## Keeping your agent happy

I have a fantastic agent. Not only is she incredibly hard-working, but she also understands and respects my side hustle. This is not the case with all agents; my agent and I got to this place because of her openness and respect for me and my respect for her and my organizational skills.

The first thing to do is talk with your agent, telling them you want to pursue corporate role play as your number one side hustle. Share that not only will it increase your earning potential, but you will also be using your acting muscles when role playing. As opposed to other side hustles, you will earn more as a role play actor, so you should be able to reduce your working hours, freeing up your time for self-taping, auditioning, line learning and taking acting classes. Share with them that acting comes first; that you will always prioritize this over role play jobs.

I have always dealt with my role play companies directly rather than via my acting agent. Most role players also do this, but some let their agent manage their role play bookings like they would an acting job. I can see that there are some benefits to this; an agent is probably more skilled than you at having 'money conversations', and if you do have a role play job that clashes with an audition or acting job, they can deal with the, probably, unhappy role play company on your behalf.

The danger is that it could damage your relationship with the role play company. I prefer to handle the heat and take comfort in knowing that I will genuinely understand the unfortunate position my cancellation may leave the role play company in. Your agent may not be this sensitive. An agent's job is to find you acting roles and build your career, which means they can sometimes look down on or devalue role play jobs.

If your agent deals with the financial side of a role play job, they will understandably take their commission. An agent's 10 or 15 per cent commission plus the VAT can remove a sizeable chunk of your earnings. One of the reasons agents are entitled to their commission is because they may be negotiating fees for you; this isn't often an option with role play fees which are often set and non-negotiable.

It is unlikely that you will be role playing more than up to twice a week in your first few years as a role player, but if you do find yourself in such demand, you need to manage your agent's expectations, ensuring them that you are still available for acting work. If they feel you are becoming less available, they may question your commitment to the industry and ask themselves whether they should keep you on their books.

I updated my agent with my role play commitments via email for years. Every week on a Monday, I would send the following email:

*Dear agents,*

*I hope this finds you well and that you had a lovely weekend.*

*Here are my upcoming role play commitments:*

*Mon 11th Sept – London, WC2 – 11am – 4pm*
*Fri 15th Sept – Oxford – all day*
*Mon 18th Sept – virtual – 9 am – 5 pm*

*Tues 19th Sept – London, EC3N – 12pm – 4pm*
*Weds 27th Sept – virtual – all day*
*Tues 3rd Oct – London, W1 – 9am – 4pm*

*Speak soon,*
*Syrus*

As you can see, I am particular about timings and locations when informing my agent of my availability. Casting Directors usually have more flexibility than they let on when scheduling audition days. I have squeezed in auditions before and after role play jobs. On rare occasions, I have even auditioned during the lunch break of a role play job. Having to be in both headspaces on the same day is not ideal, as it does require you to split your focus. But better than missing out on a day's work, upsetting the role play company or missing out on an acting audition.

I am busy with role play jobs, but I haven't had any significant clashes in the last few years due to being organized and the technological options that now afford us all. Being able to self-tape or audition virtually has massively helped in this area. I have often been able to find a spare office or break-out room to record a quick self-tape or hold a Zoom audition when on role play jobs. Be careful with this. I would only do it with role play companies and clients you know well. Most people are fine, but some may be funny about this as they are paying you for that day. I remember one old role play company boss who jibed me for running my 'office' from our role player green/break-out room. He may have had a point, but I always try to use my time effectively if there are, sometimes hours-long, significant gaps during a role play day. Like all things, make a judgement based on the relationship you have with those you are working with.

Rather than sending the previously mentioned emails, I now give my agents access to my calendar, which contains all my availability. This is much easier to manage, as role play dates and times can sometimes change. I also inform my agent if there is a role play job that I can't or would find difficult to cancel. As I now facilitate as well, I usually have a few such days a month in which this is the case, but as a new role player, this shouldn't be the case for you. In my opinion, the type of role play jobs you will be doing in your first few years are easily coverable, providing you give the role play company enough notice; more on that later. Here is what a typical week might look like on my calendar:

**September** 2023

Some acting agencies use Tagmin to manage their clients' diaries. So with your agent's permission, you could also use this platform to include your role play commitments, so all of your availability is in one place.

So, you have done everything in your power to mitigate any potential clashes, but what do you do when you have an unavoidable one? You should always prioritize the acting audition over the role play job unless the audition is ridiculously last minute or you know that cancelling the role play job may irreparably harm your relationship with the role play company. You, rather than your agent, will know the true impact of your pulling out of a particular job, whether there is a pool of role players who can step in at the last minute or if you are one of the few role players who has been briefed and rehearsed for this job.

In the past, I have not cancelled role play jobs for commercial auditions, as I had weighed up the pros and cons. Yes, the commercial may have paid me thousands of pounds, but your chances of booking commercial jobs are slim, as they audition so many actors. If the role play company is a regular employer, they could pay me a few thousand pounds in one year. I felt it wasn't worth cancelling the role play job for a last-minute commercial audition on these particular occasions.

A few years back, I was in a very tricky position when the Donmar Warehouse Theatre asked me to audition for a play. I was part of a small role play delivery team. As a team of role players, we kept suggesting to the role play company that they should train more actors up. In one sense, you could see this as doing ourselves out of work, but it came from wanting to know that if an audition came in, we would have enough actors to cover us. This is not what happened, leaving me in a challenging position. It was an audition I couldn't afford to miss, and the role play company made it clear that my cancelling would be a huge problem. That particular role play company was my number one source of income at the time. As this was an important audition due to the venue and director attached, I decided to pull out of the role play job in the most respectful way possible. The role play company was unhappy, as they had to change the job date and issued me a written warning. However, they continued to employ me for many years due to my transparency, professionalism and the hard work I put into every role play job. I became one of their primary role players and facilitators for the next ten years. Even in tricky and very awkward situations, when you think your time with a company may have ended, there may always be a positive resolution if you have a history of a good working relationship. Also, my decision here was a great example of showing my agent my unwavering commitment to my acting career.

## Keeping the role play company happy

'At React, we assume that a professional actor can act. And you can learn the skills needed, for example, to give excellent feedback to participants. But one of the most important things we look for in our team of associates is being a decent human being.

Respectful, customer focused, a 'can do' attitude, easy to work with, pleasant to our office team and the sort of person who is going to be a credit to our company when they are out on a job.'

Miles Cherry
React – Acting for Business

If it works for you and is what you want, there is no reason why you can't work for the same role play company alongside your acting career for your entire working life. I have worked for several role play companies for well over a decade. I have moved on from a small amount due to our principles no longer aligning, but generally, any moving on, on my part has been because I have outgrown the work, and my leaving was a natural progression in my role play career.

Once you begin working for a company regularly, it is worth checking in with them about how they would like you to update them on your availability. Again, like your agent, some may have a calendar system like Tagmin. Most will ask you to update them with your availability via email, monthly, bi-monthly or weekly. Set yourself a reminder and get in the habit of doing this. This type of regular communication from you will make it straightforward for them to offer you work.

Role play companies are incredibly busy, and it is easy to fall off their radars over time. I encourage you to keep checking in with them, letting them know that you are around and available for work. I have lost count of the times I have done this, and the work has started flooding in. A simple email like this will suffice:

*Dear Roleplay Company,*

*I hope this email finds you all well and having a good week.*

*I am available for any upcoming work you feel I may be suitable for.*

*Speak soon.*

*All the best,*
*Syrus*

Hopefully, as a working actor, you will have long periods when you are unavailable for role play work. Role play companies understand this. Most companies I work for want to employ role players who still work regularly in film, theatre, television and radio. Each acting job makes you a better actor. The role play company assumes you will bring this growth to the next role play job. Clients also like it when a company's role players are still working actors. In their minds, it often provides a stamp of approval to the quality of the actor, and delegates do like it when they recognize a face off the telly.

If you have an upcoming <u>confirmed</u> acting job, give the role play company advanced warning of the exact start and end dates; they will appreciate this.

There is no need to inform them of possible recalls, pencils or job offers. You want role play companies to consider you as available, making it easy for them to consider booking you.

If you are away on an acting job, as it is ending, drop the role play company an email reminding them that you will soon be available for role play work once again. There is also the possibility that you may still be able to undertake role play work while you are away on your acting job. This could be in person or virtually. I used to be the master of this, and on occasion, I probably travelled too far from London for role play jobs when I had a theatre show in the evening. I am much more cautious about this these days, as there were times when I was stretching myself too thin. This wasn't because of greed; it was often a necessity; in the past, I have appeared in some low or no paid theatre jobs, so I had no choice but to work during the day to be able to pay my bills. Even when working at some of London's most prestigious theatres, I didn't have enough left to live on after my agent's commission and my tax bill. These were cases when I was, once again, incredibly grateful to be able to top up my earnings via my role play work.

Some high-end, incredibly well-paid role play or training companies prefer to employ people who no longer work as actors. Individuals who have left the acting industry due to the lifestyle not working for them or finding other passions within their working lives. These companies value the skills that the ex-actor brings, but also, just as importantly, the ex-actor knows their availability months or even years ahead and will not cancel the role play job for an acting job.

If you are not in this place in your life, please do not work for this type of company, no matter how tempting the money is. Trust me: you will eventually come unstuck by having to let them down due to a clash with an acting job or audition. This is a moment where no matter how committed to the role play industry you are, you have to remember that it is your side hustle, and your acting career comes first. The ex-actors I know who can make this sort of commitment are incredibly busy and make an excellent living. Of course, if, in the future, things change for you career-wise, this may be a part of the industry that you do indeed want to explore.

Make sure you fully understand the role play companies' cancellation policy. Hopefully, they will have been transparent with you regarding this in your initial chat with them. If you do have to ask, bringing it up at the beginning of a new working relationship may feel awkward, but you must do so. Most companies, who prefer to employ working actors, are usually ok with you needing to pull out of a job up to two weeks before. After that, replacing you can get tricky due to other actors' availability. Sometimes, I have bitten the bullet and pulled out of a job that might clash with a *potential* recall or acting job. On some of these occasions, the recall or acting job didn't come to fruition, but at least my relationship with the role play company was still intact, as I didn't let them down at the last minute. Pulling out of a job close to the delivery date will never go down well with the company, so if you need to do this, ensure it is for an important reason. Doing this will be a judgement call for you, and most companies should hopefully understand the predicament you find yourself in. Just be honest, remind them of your professionalism, and say you would only do this in extreme cases.

When you pull out of a job, most companies will want to source a new role player themselves, but some may ask you to assist them. Your pulling out may land better if you can say that some of their other role players are available. I usually text or email some of their other actors to check their availability.

Withdrawing from a role play job due to a life emergency or illness will never be frowned upon; give them as much notice as possible. Most companies should have an out-of-hours number you can contact during such times.

One of my golden rules is to never cancel a role play job for a better-paid role play job. Again, this goes against the professionalism I encourage you to have, but I would save your brownie points. If you let a role play company down, it should be for a potentially life-changing audition or life emergency, not an extra £50.

There are occasions when the client may cancel the job. This could be for a variety of reasons. Each role play company will have a different policy regarding this. They will have an agreement with the client, which states that depending on how close the cancellation is to the actual delivery date will dictate how much the client has to pay the role play company. This, in turn, will dictate how much the role play company will pay you. This is the cancellation policy of one of the companies I currently work for:

| | |
|---|---|
| 100% of your fee | If the job is cancelled within 5 business days or under |
| 75% of your fee | If the job is cancelled between 6 – 10 business days |
| 50% of your fee | If the job is cancelled between 11 – 15 business days |
| 25% of your fee | If the job is cancelled between 16 – 20 business days |
| 0% of your fee | If the job is cancelled over 20 business days |

It gets complicated if the client postpones or moves the date. If it is a date move, the role play company will inform you immediately and ask if you are available on the new date. They will likely have to offer the date to another actor if you are unavailable. In this case, they will not be able to pay you. If it is a postponement, they will contact you when the new date is confirmed. Occasionally, a role play company has paid me for a date move I was unavailable for because the date was moved a week before the delivery date. Them paying me was right, as I was unlikely to secure another day's work at this short notice. This role play company would not have been able to charge the client for this, as they would be paying for the actor who replaced me—a sign of a company that respects its role players' time and talent.

If a role play company offers dates very far into the future, they should always caveat it with an understanding that your availability may feasibly change in six months or a year. I always accept the dates; work is work, but frame my response by saying that I am currently available and will keep them updated if my availability changes.

To echo my earlier point in 'What's in it for you – Life benefits,' I would always be careful with jobs abroad. Travelling to far-flung places to work can sound very glamorous, but you pulling out can add complications due to visas and flight and hotel bookings. Just be honest with the company; you need to fully understand how late you can pull out of this type of gig, should you need to.

The role play company should be transparent with you if an offer of work is confirmed or pencilled. A pencilled job means the client can cancel or postpone the job without being charged by the role play company. In this case, the client hasn't paid the role play company, so they won't be able to pay you. If a job is a pencil, make it clear in your diary. The role play company should have informed you when they hope to be able to confirm the job with you. At the latest, this should be around a month before the job. If another role play company offers you confirmed work, let the first company know that this is the case. Hopefully, this will put some pressure on them to confirm the job. If they cannot confirm I would take the new guaranteed job offer. The first role play company will, of course, understand why you need to do this.

You will get into the good books of a new role play company if you closely follow their payment rules. Sometimes, the role play company can only invoice the client once they have received the role players and facilitators' invoices. I would email your invoice the following day or even on the day of the job. Invoicing weekly or monthly is fine if you are doing multiple days for a company. Some role play companies will stipulate when they need your invoice, and others won't.

Most companies usually pay you within a month of you invoicing them. Some of my companies pay me immediately, some within a week, a month or even up to two months; it does vary.

Here is an example of the kind of invoice I send to role play companies:

**SYRUS LOWE**
1 The Square
Richmond
London
KT2 9JN

**Billing Address:**

Role Plays Are Us

23 Lombard Street

London

EC3V 9AA

**Date: 10/11/23**

**Invoice Number: 023RPAU**

## INVOICE

| Description | Amount |
| --- | --- |
| Zoom Rehearsal – Tuesday 26th March 2024 | £100.00 |
| Altrazert Forum Theatre session – Monday 1st April 2024 | £300.00 |
| Travel – Monday 1st April 2024 | £14.58 |
| **Total** | **£414.58** |

**Name on account: Syrus Lowe**

**Account number: 23432606**

**Sort code: 20-86-41**

Some of the larger companies I work for have dedicated reference numbers for each job and ask that I always put that reference number on my invoice. This is an easy thing to forget, trust me.

Some companies also have dedicated email accounts for you to send your invoices to. It may be something like:

invoices@roleplaycompany.com or finance@roleplaycompany.com.

Again, if they ask you to do these things, please ensure you do. If they require you to send proof of your expense receipts, you can add photos of these as attachments to your invoice.

If you work for multiple companies, it is worth using a spreadsheet or diary to track all your invoices and payments. It is easy to lose track when you get busy. I have had a few occasions when I have emailed a company about a late payment, only to find that I had yet to invoice them in the first place.

# PART THREE

# HOW TO DO IT

# CHAPTER EIGHTEEN

# How to do corporate role play

As a corporate role play actor, your job is to be a communication training tool for the participant. This will manifest differently depending on the type of role play, but that is your job. You are providing an opportunity for them to practise their communication skills. Something that people in the business world, and life generally, need to do more.

When role playing with a participant, you will be practising a conversation. More than likely a conversation with very high stakes for your character and, possibly, the participant. When practising the conversation, the participant will always be themselves; you will take on the character. The participant is never acting; that is your role. The participant may have to take on a slightly different job role or imaginary circumstances for the scenario, but they will always be having the conversation as themselves.

In real life, we open up or close down during a conversation, depending on how we feel about the other person and/or their behaviour during the interaction. The impact of their communication style will dictate how much information you share with them. In life, if you are conversing with a friend who seems genuinely interested in what's going on for you, you will tell them more. Conversely, when you talk to someone, such as a sibling, who seems distracted and disinterested during your conversation, you will naturally share less with them. A helpful thing to start practising during your real-life conversations moving forwards is to begin to analyse how they and the person you are conversing with make you feel. What behavioural things do they demonstrate that encourage you to engage with them? What do they do that makes you want the conversation to end?

In most role play scenarios, the participant will be trying to uncover what is going on for your character, so they can assist you in making your character's situation better. These may be circumstances concerning your character's professional or personal life. Getting this information out of you will require the participant to deploy the most effective communication skills needed for that conversation.

Role play sessions vary significantly; they can be anything from five to thirty minutes, with some bespoke role plays or forum theatre sessions lasting up to an hour. No matter the length of the role play, the communication skills that the participant needs to demonstrate are always the same. Forum theatre only partially follows these rules; I will explain why when we get to it.

So from an Actor's POV here are my top tips when doing roleplay/forum work:

- Learn to listen double. When roleplaying as your character make sure you're aware of the learning involved. Listening to the facilitator and more so, listening to participant suggestions, while also staying in character. Listen to the scene, the learning and the suggestions. Easier said than done.
- Learning is the key. Make sure you're fully aware of the learning that needs to be delivered. What the client wants their employees to walk away with. Which skills, techniques and ideas are you helping to deliver. Yes, you're an actor, and you're being truthful to the role. But with roleplay, you're also a communicator in training.
- Be malleable. Suggestions and changes will come fast from participants and facilitators alike. Be ready and prepared to understand and switch tactic very quickly (especially when in character).
- Don't be afraid. The facilitator will manage the whole situation. The learning, the roleplay, and what you need to. Relax and know you will be guided.

> - Finally, be a team player in the room. Know your lines, know the learning, and know the client you're roleplaying for.
> - (Oh, and be ready to be surprised by participant suggestions. Anything could be said)'
>
> Mitesh Soni
> Actor

Here are the primary communication skills you should respond to, in character, during any role play conversation. You react to them as you would in a real-life conversation; if the participant is using them successfully, you give them more information and less if they are not.

# Rapport building

For most role plays, the participant should be engaging in some level of rapport building with your character at the start of the conversation. Rapport building can last as little as thirty seconds or even up to a few minutes. It would be strange for someone to start interrogating you about your personal life when they had not already established a relationship with you.

Due to nervousness, many participants will skip this all-important section. They often panic about the fact that there are time constraints and want to get straight to uncovering what your character's issue is. When they do this, they have missed a key learning point of the role play, as rapport building is an essential component of effective communication.

Good rapport building starts with them entirely focused on you. They should say hello, use your character's name, say they are looking forward to talking with you, thank you for your time and ask you an excellent rapport-building question such as:

- How are you today?

- Where have you come in from today?

- How is your day going?

- How was your weekend?

- How are your family?

- How is your morning going so far?

I know these sound like simple things that we all do naturally, day in, day out, but, as I said, the participant's nerves will mean they often skip this. This has happened to me countless times when I have been role playing.

The other common thing is for them to ask you a good rapport question, for you to answer it, and then ask them a follow-up rapport question, only for them to ignore it, not reply, and dive into chasing your character's issue. The participant should be listening and responding to you at all times. You asking them a question and them not answering is not a great start to a conversation. They should be willing to engage in as much rapport building as your character is happy to do.

Don't get me wrong; there may be times when your character may not want to engage in rapport due to the pressure of the character's issue or their personality. If this is the case, your role play brief will state this. In this situation, the participant should listen, observe and respond to your needs and get straight to what you want to discuss.

If the participant demonstrates good rapport behaviour at the start of the interaction, you will be more open to discussing your issue with them. If they have not done this, you will not be starting from a place of openness, and it is helpful for the participants learning to see this demonstrated in your behaviour. The participant will hopefully pick up on this and adjust their communication style. Practical ways to let the participant know that their lack of rapport building impacted you negatively at the beginning of a role play include:

- Give them short or one-word answers when they ask you a question.

- Not engaging in eye contact. I have done role plays where I have spent the whole time looking at the floor or towards the door because the participant has made me feel so uncomfortable.

- Having very closed body language.

- Minimizing your issue by saying things such as: '*I'm not sure this is that important*', '*Maybe I'm blowing this out of proportion*', or '*I think I can handle this myself.*'
- Verbalizing that you feel they may not be the right person for you to speak to.
- Physicalizing that you feel uncomfortable by tapping your foot, fidgeting or moving around in your seat.
- Stumbling over your words or getting tongue-tied.
- Looking like you are close to tears.

## Framing the conversation

A successful role play will start with you being clear about why you are there and having this particular conversation now. I describe this as framing the conversation, ensuring that both parties are in the picture about the conversation. You will, of course, have read your role play brief, so you will know when doing the role play if the participant has explained this to your character adequately. The participant should share why the conversation is happening and then check that what they have said makes sense to you.

Suppose the participant does not frame the conversation. In that case, your character will need clarification. Again, you can express this via your body language, eye contact, or even by asking them to clarify what this meeting is about.

There are some role plays where the participant will have no idea what the conversation is about, so they cannot frame it as such. But they can still engage in rapport and tell you that this is your time to talk and that they are here to listen.

## Active Listening

This is a big one, and one of the things that many participants do not excel at during role plays – genuinely listening and responding to what you are saying and showing them. Most participants are nervous during role play, especially at the start. Their heads are full of the content of their delegate briefs. They may also feel the pressure of being observed by a facilitator or examiner, so actively listening to you can become challenging.

A good participant will give you the time and space to respond to them. They should ask you questions and leave the appropriate gap for you to reply. They should not be talking at you in a never-ending monologue, cutting you off while you are speaking, or asking you a question and then answering it themselves. They should also be giving you the time to formulate your answers and thoughts and potentially make certain indicative non-verbal sounds, which will let you know that they are listening to you; the occasional nodding or shaking of the head may accompany these sounds.

Another clear sign they are genuinely listening to you is by being able to summarize what you have said. If they can repeat verbatim what you shared with them, they clearly were listening to you. An excellent introduction to their summary may sound like this:

- 'So if I am clear, what you have just said is ...'

- 'Just so we are both on the same page, I would like to repeat back what I have heard you say ...'

- 'So what you're saying is ...'

- 'Before we move on, let me summarize what I think I heard you say ...'

Once they have summarized, they should check in to ensure you agree with what they said. Ensuring you are both on the same page before the conversation moves on.

The participant using exact words or phrases you have used in their follow-up question is another clear sign of brilliant active listening.

QaQa (also known as linear or socratic questioning) is a wonderful technique I discovered on my role play journey. QaQa is Question, answer, Question, answer ...

The participant should ask you a question, and you then answer it; the participant's next question should be a follow on from the answer you have just given them, not a random question they have decided to ask you.

A QaQa conversation might look something like this:

| | |
|---|---|
| Participant | *'Tell me how the project is going.'* |
| Role Player | *'Yeah, we are getting there. It has turned out to be a lot more work than we had planned, particularly the initial audit.'* |
| Participant | *'Why has the initial audit been more work than you anticipated?'* |
| Role Player | *'I think we just misunderstood the scope of it. Whenever we thought we had reached the end, we discovered a new area that needed analysis. This created a lot of stress and pressure on the team.'* |
| Participant | *'Describe what that stress and pressure looked like?'* |

As you can see, each follow-up question is dictated by and responds to the previous answer.

This **Participant** is actively listening to the **Role Player** in the moment, building on what they have just said and shared with them, not being influenced by their own assumptions, pre-judgements or personal biases.

QaQa is another helpful tool to practise during daily conversations to help you sharpen your active listening skills. Put yourself in the participant's place and dare yourself to only ask follow-up questions about things that have just been shared with you by the person you are talking to.

If a participant uses the QaQa technique, they will be on your character's agenda rather than enforcing their own. Essentially pulling the information out of you, rather than pushing onto you, what they think your character is feeling, thinking, or what they think your character should do.

The job roles of many of the delegates you will be role playing with require them to be solution focused, identifying a problem and fixing it as quickly as possible so they can move on to the next task. Role play conversations require them to do the opposite, to slow their thinking down so they fully absorb all you are saying, showing and doing. The beginning of most role play conversations should be them finding out what is going on for your character before moving into any conversations around solutions or next steps. QaQa is the perfect technique to ensure they do this and do not get ahead of themselves.

If the delegate's active listening skills could be better, then it is your job to let them know. You can respond by displaying discomfort, annoyance or even anger, whichever feels most appropriate. Common examples of bad active listening skills include:

- Cutting you off while you are speaking

- Rushing you

- Talking over you

- Finishing your sentences for you

- Talking about what they think your issue is rather than listening to you

- Moving onto another subject when you are displaying that you want to stay on the current one

- Not giving you the time to answer their questions

- Asking you a question and answering it themselves

- Not using your exact words and phrases when reflecting on what you have just shared with them

- Talking about themselves or their issues

- Not picking up on cues or hooks you mention more than once

This is a great learning and development area for many delegates, and for all of us in life, so it is worth reminding you what good active listening looks like.

If they are actively listening to you, you will see and hear the following:

- Space and time before and after you have spoken

- Not talking over you

- Not cutting you off when you are speaking

- Not answering their questions themselves

- Encouraging non-verbal sounds
- Body language, such as nodding or shaking their heads
- Summarizing what you have shared with them
- Use your exact words or phrases in their next question
- QaQa
- Not rushing to solutions

# Silence

Silence, which I also refer to as thinking time, or space is imperative during a good role play. It is essential for your character to have the space and time to formulate their thoughts; this fundamentally requires silence. The delegates also need that time to digest what you have said and work out where they want to take the conversation next. There is also the possibility that you may have shared something, left a small gap to breathe or think, and were about to share some more, and then the delegate goes and cuts you off. If the delegate is always jumping in when you leave the gap, they will never fully hear everything your character wants to share.

Silence is one of the areas in which many delegates struggle. Not only delegates but many of us find silence during a conversation awkward. The slightest gap can make us wonder where to take the conversation next or if what we say is interesting or relevant. We all must improve at embracing and holding the silence; it is incredibly powerful if done well.

Ideally, there should be congruence between the delegate's use of silence and the rest of what they're communicating; gentle body language, stillness and focused eye contact all work incredibly well alongside silence. The silence gives you the thinking time to formulate your answers. If your character is emotional, they may need this time. A delegate giving you the appropriate amount of silence during a role play should be rewarded massively by you giving them more information. You should also share with them how helpful their use of silence was for your character during the feedback section.

When feeding back on silence, I often share with delegates that in a conversation, they should '*let the silence do the heavy lifting*.'

# Eye contact

The participant's level of eye contact with you is another simple way of working out if they are genuinely engaging with and speaking to you. Are they looking at you? Are they looking at you for the majority of the time? Or are their eyes darting around the room, looking everywhere but your face?

When participants are nervous, distracted or unprepared, their eye contact is often one of the first things to suffer. What they need to do is gain your characters' trust before you share your issues with them; their avoidance of your eyes will not help in this respect.

I have played vulnerable role play characters who struggle to maintain eye contact with people. In these circumstances, the participant should maintain good eye contact with me to encourage me to open up and trust them. I have had very successful role plays where I started with my eyes focused solely on the floor. Due to the delegates' warmth, patience and care, my character eventually found the confidence to look them in the eyes when talking.

If my character doesn't have the above eye contact challenges and the participant is not maintaining a good amount of eye contact with me, I will mirror their level of eye contact and, probably once again, be very limited with the amount of information I share.

# Body language

As actors, we are generally highly aware of the impact of body language; we can watch a play or a film and, without hearing the words, can probably work out how the characters feel about their situation and each other. This principle applies in a business setting, too; I think you can walk past an occupied office, be unable to hear the conversation, and still be able to work out the dynamics between those inside just by their body language.

In a role play setting, if a delegate has open body language, it will open you and your thinking up, encouraging you to share more with them. This good practice will also impact your body language; you will, essentially, mirror their body language; if they are open with you, you will be open with them.

If the delegate's body language is closed, it will have the opposite effect on you; it will close you down, and you may even sit not facing them.

Their body language may change during the role play; if it does, you should adjust yours too. Participants do tend to improve as role plays progress. Suppose the delegate has the emotional intelligence to realize that their body language has a negative impact on you, and they adjust it. You should reward their positive behaviour by changing yours.

Things to look out for when it comes to body language are:

- Are they facing you straight on?

- Is their chest and torso open and upright?

- Are their hand gestures calm and open or aggressive and choppy?

- Are their feet facing you or facing in another direction?

- Are they fidgeting or playing with a pen, the desk or a notepad?

- How still are they?

- Do they appear entirely focused on you?

- Are they smiling at you, and are their facial expressions soft and relaxed?

- Is there anything about their body language indicating they seem uncomfortable, unprepared or nervous?

## Pace of speech

I am sure we have all been in situations where the importance of an event, where we have to speak, has made us talk much faster than usual. It makes sense; if you are feeling uncomfortable in a situation, you will want it to be over as soon as possible so you speak more quickly.

Due to nerves, this often happens to participants during role plays. This fast-paced speech will always have a negative impact on you. If the participant is speaking too fast, the effect on you is that it may make you feel rushed, hurried, unimportant and potentially confused. You can, of course, reflect on this during the feedback session, but you can also indicate and embody this feeling during a role play in the following way:

- Asking the delegate to repeat what they have said.
- Show confusion via your facial expressions.
- Use your body language to disengage from the participant and the conversation.
- Display that you are struggling to keep up with what they are saying.
- Saying, 'I didn't quite understand that', or 'Could you take me through that again.'
- Attempting to speak or respond and then shutting down when they continue to talk over you.
- Cut off your eye contact while you try to process what they said.

As role players, we respond this way, hoping that the participants will pick up on this and adjust their communication style.

## Conversation percentage

Generally, your character should be doing most of the talking during role play conversations. The participant should be asking you effective open-ended questions, enabling them to get as much information from you as possible. They, of course, can share their insights and input, but these should be secondary to yours. I would say that a perfect role play conversation should consist of the following:

Seventy per cent you talking
Thirty per cent them talking

Delegates over-talking and not giving you the space and time to think and speak during a role play is very common. It is incredible how long I have been talked <u>at</u> during a role play rather than being brought into the conversation and asked probing questions.

Once again, this is a great subject to bring up during the feedback session, but during the role play, feel free to look bored, disinterested, distracted or annoyed if you think they are talking too much.

## Tone of voice

A delegate's tone of voice is another hugely impactful element of what will open you up or close you down during a role play conversation.

I am sure you have heard the saying, 'It's not what you say, but how you say it'. This is never truer than when it comes to tone of voice. A delegate can be saying all of the right things to you, but if their tone doesn't match their words, if they are not congruent, it will probably not sound genuine or sincere. I have been in feedback sessions with participants after a role play who were perplexed as to why their words did not have their desired impact on me. I explained that it was to do with their tone of voice, I verbally replayed how I heard them during the interaction, and then shared the effect it had on me.

Many people need to be made aware of how their voices sound and its impact on others. How you sound, and your tone of voice are habitual behaviours and are often the result of several emotional, psychological and societal factors. Most people use a tiny fraction of their vocal range and do not realize they can shift and play with their vocal tone or voice depending on the conversation and who they are talking to. Funnily enough, most pet owners do this naturally when talking to their animals. Because the animals do not understand the content of what they are saying, the owner puts more inflexion, emotion and range into their voice to communicate with their pet.

A good role play delegates tone of voice should sound warm, inviting, calm, curious, empathetic, caring, genuine, engaged or patient. It shouldn't sound harsh, judgemental, aggressive, disinterested, choppy, fake, intimidating or insincere.

# Questions

## *Open questions*

You cannot answer an open question with a yes or no response. When asked an open question, you are inclined to give a more detailed answer. An open question can only start with one of six words:

- Who
- What
- Why
- Where
- When
- How

I describe them as your five *Wh*'s and your *How*.

Open questions open up your thinking and responses, encouraging you to give more detailed answers.

Closed questions can close your thinking down and limit your responses. A closed question can start with many different words, including:

- Is
- Could
- Should
- Did
- Will
- Are
- Can
- Was
- Do

I am not saying that closed questions are wrong and that delegates should never use them. They are helpful to the delegates when they need to clarify their understanding of what you have shared. In fact, in medical role plays, when well-balanced with some open questions, closed questions can be handy to eliminate or discount what a patient's problem might be.

During a role play, especially at the start, the participant should lean towards open questions rather than closed ones. They are usually on a fact-finding mission to uncover what is going on for your character; in this instance, open questions are their best friends.

Again, I encourage you to start your role player learning journey now. Begin to tune in and listen to the types of questions you and those around you ask. I guarantee that you will hear many closed questions.

You may also hear questions where they are forcing options onto you, such as:

● 'Is it this or is it that?'

● 'Did that happen, or was it this?'

● 'Was it him or was it her?'

We can often flip these questions into open ones. Take the above three:

● 'What is it?'

● 'What happened?'

● 'Who was it?'

We, as humans, don't know what the person we are talking to will say, so why limit their thinking by forcing options upon them? Let them share what they want to share.

You may also hear leading questions, which are basically the participant's opinions disguised as questions:

● Do you think that maybe you should have another look at that proposal?

● Do you think it might be a good idea to speak to Derek about the floor reallocation?

- Have you thought that maybe you're not ready for promotion?

Business communication training focuses heavily on open and closed questions, so the concept of these should be familiar to the participants. If they are consistently asking you closed questions, it is helpful for you to respond with a yes, no or a one-word answer. Hopefully, they should pick up on this and start to use more open-ended questions.

As a general rule of thumb, if the participant asks short open questions, you should respond with long-detailed answers. If they ask long, complicated, closed questions full of their assumptions and opinions, you will not be inclined to provide particularly comprehensive responses. Long closed questions are another example of delegates pushing their agenda onto you, trying to control the conversation, rather than listening and responding to what you are showing and saying to them.

Another common tendency is for delegates to ask you multiple questions, firing one after another at you. This often happens because they are trying to work out what they want to ask you while talking rather than pausing, taking a breath, formulating the question in their head and then asking you that question. If they ask you multiple questions, I encourage you to answer the question you want to or answer the last one. Feel free to act confused by the number of questions they ask. Naturally, you can only respond to one question at a time. Once again, the hope is that they will notice the impact the closed or multiple questions have on you and adjust the questions they are asking. In my experience, when they ask you multiple questions, the first question is usually the right and most impactful one; it is usually an open question in response to what you have just shared with them. But they lose confidence in that question and end up firing more, usually closed questions, at you. They should ask you a short open question and then leave a gap to give you time to formulate your response.

I have acted in role play scenarios where the delegate has not asked me one question. These were role play conversations where the delegates' job was to discover what was going on for my character, and they just talked at me. The role play actor's job is to respond as you would in a real-life conversation. In a situation like this, that response may be complete silence, closed body language, appearing uncomfortable or, if I feel (as the character) confident enough, challenging their approach by saying that I would like to speak or share my thoughts.

## TED questions

Another type of question you should reward by giving lots of information to the delegates are TED questions. They are slightly more like instructions but are incredibly powerful for opening up your thinking and getting you to think more deeply. The T stands for tell, the E for explain and the D for describe. The TED questions start with:

- Tell
- Explain
- Describe

If their questions start with one of these three words, you should give them a more detailed answer. The great thing about the TED questions is that they lead into the open questions:

- Tell me when
- Tell me how
- Tell me who
- Explain to me why that was
- Explain what was going on there
- Explain how that happened
- Describe how you felt
- Describe what that looked like
- Describe where you were that day

When the delegates ask you TED questions, they pull the information out of you rather than push their agenda onto you. Being asked TED questions requires you to paint a picture of what is going on for your character, provide more detail and be more honest with your responses. TED questions also need space around them; the delegate is potentially asking you personal things, so you need the space and silence to think about how you want to respond. Ultimately the delegate, via their communication skills, needs to make you feel psychologically safe.

The ability to confidently ask TED questions, and leave that space, are quite advanced communication skills, so I encourage you to reward the participant by giving them lots of information and possibly even share with them that it is nice for you to be able to speak about these things so openly and to feel safe in doing so. Reflecting congruently with your body language, facial expressions, and general positive engagement is also helpful.

I first discovered TED questions when working as a role player opposite police officers. Over the years, I have done numerous role plays with police officers, playing victims, suspects, witnesses and children. Police officers use a lot of TED questions, as they need extensive, broad and detailed answers when they are asking you to describe a crime scene, a suspect, a weapon or a day that may be very distant in your memory.

Each profession uses different questions depending on what they are trying to achieve. The one thing they all have in common is that the questions asked are a choice, learnt over many years via training and experience doing their job, rather than one they use due to habitual behaviour.

Councillors and therapists will predominantly ask open questions, as they are trained to open up your thinking and potentially try to enable you to find your own solutions.

A doctor may start with an open question but then ask you a series of closed questions as they try to diagnose you and funnel out things that don't apply. Doctors are also usually time-pressured, so closed questions are the most efficient to keep the patient on track.

A slightly more manipulative approach to open and closed questions comes from the world of barristers. They may ask their witnesses a series of closed questions to keep them on track but may ask the opposing side's witnesses many open questions to get them talking and thus potentially tie themselves up in knots.

In an interview setting, the person interviewing should be very aware of the types of questions they are using; open questions to explore and closed questions to clarify.

Politicians have a slightly odd relationship with open and closed questions, because they sometimes try to avoid giving direct answers. The interviewer will ask the politician a closed question requiring a yes or no response. The politician will skilfully find a way of responding as if they have been asked an open question, therefore avoiding having to give a direct answer. This happens day in and day out on the news. There is a famous clip from the BBC programme *Newsnight* where the presenter Jeremy Paxman asks the then-conservative politician Michael Howard the same closed question: '*Did you threaten to overrule him?*' twelve times! Michael Howard responds slightly differently each time, never answering the question directly. This behaviour is not to be encouraged in a role play setting. Still, it is an excellent example of both Paxman and Howard making deliberate choices regarding their questioning technique and responses.

Children are the most prolific users of open questions; they love using open questions because they are curious and constantly want to learn and expand their knowledge. Generally, they are particularly fond, as many parents will know, of the one-word open question 'Why?'.

This child-like level of curiosity is what the delegates should have during a role play. In my experience, most of them don't. They should be operating from this level of curiosity, but their opinions, assumptions and biases often block them.

Generally, they should ask you the correct questions to make you feel safe enough to share what is happening for your character. If they do most of the talking, they will probably not discover what your character is going through or needs.

## Empathy

A participant showing and displaying empathy is often essential during a role play brief. If the participant truly wants you to open up and share what is going on for your character, they must show that they are aware of your feelings and point of view. They, of course, cannot pretend to understand what you have gone through but can indicate that they are there for you now. All of the positive behaviours described in this chapter fall under empathetic behaviour.

Powerful empathetic phrases which will have a positive impact on you include:

- I can see this is hard for you.

- I am so sorry that you are currently dealing with this.

- I can hear how difficult it is for you to share this.

- Thank you for trusting me by telling me this.

- Let me know if you want to take a break or get some fresh air.

- I can see this upsetting you; let me know if you want some tissues.

A helpful description of empathy is, putting yourself in someone else's shoes.

Another great way a participant can show empathy is by sharing a story or a time when they or someone they know has experienced something similar to what you are experiencing. They, of course, should not hijack the conversation or start to make it about them, but letting you know that you are not the only person who has gone through what you are currently going through will be incredibly impactful for your character.

With regards to all of the skills in this chapter:

Rapport building
Framing the conversation
Active listening
Silence
Eye contact
Body language
Pace of speech
Conversation percentage
Tone of voice
Open and TED questions
Empathy

Delegates may improve during a ten, twenty or thirty-minute role play. If they do you should adjust your responses and reward their improved communication skills by giving them more information.

While we are on timings, many role play conversations will not get to an end or conclusion. Please do not place extra pressure on yourself to feel that you need to tie the conversation up like in the end of a film. Remember that a role play is a practice conversation, a chance for a practice or an assessment of the participant's communication skills. The actual role play is just a mechanism for this to happen, so some shorter role play conversations may only consist of the beginning of a conversation or particularly crucial moment.

The final thing is that there may be times when you, as the role player, may be in charge of the timekeeping element of a role play. If it is a *training* role play, there may be a bit more flexibility on the timings, and if you run over by a few minutes, it is not the end of the world. It is better to try and let the role play come to a natural conclusion rather than cutting the participant off mid-sentence.

If it is an assessment role play, it must end on time. Giving participants extra time, even thirty seconds, can give them an unfair advantage.

If a facilitator, trainer or assessor is in the room with you, they would usually look after the timekeeping element so that you can focus on the role play.

# CHAPTER NINETEEN

# How to give feedback

'Well done is how I like my steak – that is not feedback!'
A facilitator I worked with in 2014

Good acting skills are essential for any successful corporate role play actor, but your feedback skills are as necessary. Providing clear feedback to a participant after a role play is a vital role player skill that will get you employed repeatedly.

It is a role player's superpower. The delegates will expect you to be a good actor whose acting skills enable them to think that the role play is a real conversation, allowing them to invest in it fully. They are often surprised when the actor can also provide them with actionable, clear and detailed feedback. I have been in a few situations when, after giving feedback, the delegate said, '*How do you know all of that? I thought you were just an actor!*' I have never taken this negatively; they are often surprised when you can convincingly inhabit their world and deliver brilliant feedback. The general public can forget that the actor is always interested in the human condition and the behaviours that go along with it.

As with all of these things, practice makes you better. I will not say perfect, as there is always more to learn and new challenges when providing feedback to delegates. I am still learning and stealing feedback techniques from my role play colleagues and facilitators, and I have been giving feedback for twenty years!

I promise you that your feedback will get better and better. You will begin to find ease when delivering post-role play feedback. I auditioned for a role play company many years ago and struggled to provide feedback after the role play audition. I couldn't recall enough clear things that had happened during the role play. Back then, feedback was still relatively new to me, and the pressure of an audition situation probably impacted my feedback ability on the day. That particular role play company must have seen promise in me; I attended a few of their training sessions, and they eventually took me on. I worked with them for many years after that. They didn't pay me to attend their training sessions, but, for me, it was a worthwhile long-term investment. Remember that running these training sessions will always be at a cost to the role play company; they may have to pay for a venue, lunch and role players to role play with you.

Most role play companies who want new talent, talent who are new to role play, will not expect you to be experts in giving feedback. If you are in a casting bracket they want to fill and they see you demonstrate believable acting, focus, passion and attention to detail; they will invest in you and assume that with guidance and training, your feedback skills will improve over time.

To 'act' in a role play and simultaneously log the feedback is hard work; it requires laser-sharp focus and intense observational skills.

Before I get into the delivery of role play feedback, I want to talk about transitioning from the character you are playing in the role play to the professional role play actor sharing feedback. This, at times, can be challenging, especially if your character was emotional, angry or upset. Or if your character felt a degree of venom or animosity towards the delegate during the role play. You mustn't carry this emotion into the feedback section. There needs to be a clear dividing line between these two session elements. This was one of the things those new to role play found most challenging when I ran my role play masterclass. They were probably so invested in the acting during the role play they got caught up in the emotion; it is a delicate balance, which we all find over time. A few things that I think can help with this transitional period include the following:

- Having a clear beat between you finishing the role play and starting the feedback section.

- A deep breath in and out after the role play; the delegate will probably breathe with you, which helps settle their nerves before they hear your feedback.

- A big wide smile from you indicates that the intensity of the role play has now finished, and you are now both moving into the developmental feedback section.

- Take a sip of water.

- Verbalizing and labelling what is happening by saying something like:

  '*Ok, John, the role play has now finished; I am no longer Barry; I am back to being Syrus.* (smile) *We will now move into the feedback section and talk about what just happened.*'

The delegate needs to see and feel this switch in you. It will help put them at ease and not muddy the waters between the two sections. It will also help you appear more confident and grounded, no matter how nervous you feel.

'Try not to underestimate that giving and receiving personal, specific feedback constructively and objectively is a skill and is also most likely WAY out of their comfort zone. It's easy to forget this, as we are so used to being amongst fellow actors and those who are comfortable with stretching themselves.

You may find that the change for the client comes after they have processed the learning, had time to self-reflect and having observed their peers both inside and outside of the room.'

Shamia Chalabi
Actor

Now, I would like to define what I mean by giving feedback: not always, but often, after a role play, you will tell the delegate how certain things they did, certain behaviours they demonstrated, made you feel during the role play and provide them with feedback on how their communication style and choices impacted you. This is a fantastic learning opportunity for them, as they rarely get such feedback from those on the receiving end of their communication style.

The facilitator or trainer may only ask you for your feedback; they may also provide their observations and ask the delegate for feedback on themselves. You may deliver your feedback and leave the room or stay for the whole conversation. It will vary from job to job and facilitator to facilitator. If there is a facilitator or trainer, make sure you are clear about what type of feedback they would like you to deliver, how much, and how much time you have to do it.

If no facilitator or trainer is present, you will effectively run the room and manage the feedback section.

## You are providing the delegate with evidence-based developmental feedback

It is evidence-based because it has happened, and you both experienced it.

It is developmental because you share it with them to help improve their communication skills.

Giving delegates feedback requires a great deal of sensitivity. The delegates are often in a vulnerable state following a role play. They have been pushed out of their comfort zone and are often quite nervous about the feedback they will receive. For this reason, it must be delivered with care, be evidence-based and not just your opinion.

The following framework will keep your feedback evidence-based, and if the delegates don't agree with your feedback, this framework should prevent the delegate from getting too defensive.

> When you ...
>
> I felt ...

The 'When you' is the action the delegate did. It may be a physical action or the words they used.

The 'I felt' is how you felt as a result of their actions.

No matter how much the delegate may disagree with your feedback, they cannot disagree with your feelings. Whether the delegate intended it or not, it is how you felt.

It is helpful to be very precise with your language here. I would avoid the phrase '*you made me feel*', as they can push back on this by saying they didn't mean to make you feel that way. The safer and more neutral language is to say, '*I felt*'.

It is rare for a delegate to challenge your feedback, but should it happen, this framework will keep your feedback factual and evidence-based rather than slipping into your opinions.

Here are some examples of what this feedback framework might look like:

> When you opened the door and welcomed me into the room, I felt relaxed and safe.

> When you looked at your phone three times during the role play, I felt devalued and as if I was taking up your time.

> When you asked me a series of open questions, I felt listened to and comfortable sharing my story with you.

> When you spoke over me three times during the role play, I felt annoyed and unimportant.

As you can see, the participant cannot deny all of the above 'when you' statements, even if they don't remember doing it.

Here are some examples of unhelpful feedback statements:

> *When you thought I was making up excuses for my lateness, I felt undermined* – this is not helpful because you can't prove what they thought.

> *When you didn't want to have this conversation with me, I felt incredibly sad* – you can't prove they didn't want to have the conversation with you. It would be best if you shared with them what they did and the behaviours that indicated to you that they may not have wanted to have the conversation with you.

*When you started to talk about your own problems, it was like you felt your problems were more important than mine* – firstly, your 'I felt' should be about your feelings and not the participants. You also can't prove what the participant felt, only what you observed them do.

It is all about keeping it factual and evidence-based. Your choice of words is imperative as the participant will be hanging on your every word. Once again, I encourage you to start practising this daily. Observe your conversations with friends, family, cashiers and people in the park. Even if you don't verbalize the feedback, think about how you would frame it if you provided them with evidence-based developmental feedback.

As you start your role player journey, sharing three bits of feedback is enough. Providing three bits of solid evidence-based feedback is better than a long list of vague statements or opinions.

I would aim to share two positive things the participant did well.

You may find you have just completed a role play and are struggling to come up with anything positive to say, but it is essential that you do. No matter how bad you felt they were, they must feel they did some things well.

The other piece of feedback should be developmental, something they could have done differently that would have had a better impact on you.

'When giving feedback, it is vital to be kind and leave participants feeling motivated. Assume that, like most of us, they are doing their best. Always share more positives than growth areas and give the positives real weight – in the words you use, tone of voice and your body language. We can all show off about how many development points we've noticed, but overloading people with things to fix is more likely to demoralise them. Just prioritise the top one or two things that you think they will practically be able to work on and leave the rest.'

Kate Copeland
Facilitator and Business Actor

I know that some actors can find providing feedback to participants intimidating. Especially those participants who have high-powered jobs, are seemingly knowledgeable and work in an industry you know very little about. You, the actor, are the communication expert. You have just experienced the interaction with the participant. You are the most qualified person in the room to provide in-the-moment feedback. Any nerves you feel during your first few times giving feedback will dissipate as you and your feedback grow in confidence.

As this confidence takes shape, you can be free to build the amount of feedback you share with the participant as your ability to engage in a role play and log the feedback will dramatically improve. I urge you never to overload a participant with too much feedback. Think about when you have received feedback from a director or teacher; you can only take so much on board at a time. Suppose I find myself in situations where I could provide endless feedback. In that case, I always choose the feedback I think will significantly impact the participant's communication style if they can change it. What is going to make them become a more empathetic communicator? What is achievable for them over time? And remember, it's not only about the things they need to change; it's also about what they are doing well and should keep doing.

The areas you should provide the delegate with feedback on are the ones you were responding to during the role play:

Rapport building
Framing the conversation
Active listening
Use of silence
Eye contact
Body language
Pace of speech
Conversation percentage
Tone of voice
Open questions
TED questions
Empathy

If you are asked to describe how you were made to feel during an interaction, resist the urge to generalise or make sweeping statements.

Use specific examples to explain the emotion that was triggered using direct, verbatim quotes, a particular tone of voice which was used, different behaviours demonstrated or exact body language examples.

This ensures that active listening and memory recall works both ways in communication development.

Evidence-based feedback creates immediate value for the learning and enhances buy-in and trust in the process.'

Michelle Morris
Actor Coach/Facilitator

As I have been delivering feedback for a long time, I tend to make my feedback sessions more conversational to enable me to gain insights from the participant. Again, I don't feel that you should explore this at the beginning of your journey, but knowing that this might be an option in the future is helpful. I will share a helpful framework for this feedback style in the 'Bespoke role play' chapter.

It is also important that you are modelling the behaviour you are talking about when you give feedback. So when you share feedback, keep an eye on your use of silence, eye contact, body language, pace of speech, tone of voice and level of empathy.

Another helpful thing to have in your feedback tool kit is the idea of:

## Intention vs impact

This is the idea that the delegate may have intended one thing when they communicated with you, but the impact on you was different. Intention versus impact is another way to keep your feedback neutral and reinforce the idea of the 'I felt' being about your feelings, which they cannot argue with. So, during the feedback, you can share that you know it wasn't their intention, but the impact on you was different.

Please don't be offended if your feedback shocks or disheartens the participant. This may be the first time they have heard a particular piece of feedback, or it may be the tenth. Either way, they may need time to process what you have said, which may need to be after your session with them. If this does happen, take comfort that you have done your job correctly, professionally and fairly.

You may also have to judge how sensitively you need to deliver your feedback. I have gone to give feedback in the past to people who are shaking with fear. Sometimes the role play experience has just been too much for them or triggered some past trauma. You are not a therapist, a councillor or a facilitator, so please do not stray into taking on any of these roles. On these occasion not giving any feedback at all may be the best thing, Just trust your judgement and remember that this is a learning opportunity for the participant, and the environment should be a safe one at all times.

Occasionally, you may be required to provide written feedback. This may be instead of or in addition to the verbal feedback. This is usually because it is an assessment role play, and the role play element is only one part of the assessment. At the end of the assessment process, the assessors will review all of the candidate's feedback and decide their fate. This conversation may happen after you have left for the day or even at the end of the week. When asked to provide written feedback, you will respond to specific questions, such as:

How did the candidate make you feel at the start of the conversation?

How comfortable did you feel sharing your story with the candidate?

How confident were you that the candidate would handle your situation moving forward?

Do you feel you made the right choice speaking to the candidate?

As you can see, you can still weave in the communication areas I have previously mentioned, but your answers need to be in response to the specific questions on the form. Remember that even with the written form, it is a case of explaining what they did and how you felt. Or how you felt during the role play and why. You are always keeping it evidence-based.

The candidate may have access to your written feedback. If it is an assessment exam, they have paid a lot of money for and failed; the candidate may request to see their feedback to understand why they failed and how they can improve next time. If the candidate disputes the decision of the exam decision makers, the candidate and/or those reviewing their case may request to see your feedback. I am highlighting these points to remind you to keep your written feedback professional, evidence-based and never personal.

'You have to have two hats on simultaneously; one being a believable and responsive actor, the other noticing and remembering the specific things the person is doing so you can share that feedback with them. If you want to and it's appropriate, make notes in character.

Be specific. To help the person opposite you get the most out of this experience; you want to articulate what they did and what impact it had. What type of questions were they using? What was their eye contact like? How fast did they speak? Evidential and impact-led feedback is gold dust.'

Lizzie Twells
Actor

Over the years, I have developed, or probably stolen, some useful phrases to help my feedback land positively with participants. They can sometimes be in a vulnerable place after a role play, and these phrases can help soften your feedback:

'Well done for going first' – if there is more than one participant role playing that day, I will always congratulate the person who goes first. I praise them for their bravery and showing the other participants that partaking in the role play wasn't as scary as they might have thought.

'This is an unreal situation; if you can do it here, you can do it anywhere' – I acknowledge that they are role playing and having a fictional conversation with an actor, someone they have never met before. If they have the courage and confidence to do it with me, they can do it with their colleagues at work.

'I wonder what would have happened if ...' – this is a lovely way to ease yourself into developmental feedback. It can sometimes feel like quite a sharp turn when you have to move from positive to developmental feedback. Phrases like this frame the developmental feedback as options rather than them feeling like they did something wrong.

'What could have been done differently ...' – again framing the developmental feedback as an option. I acknowledge that they made one choice during the conversation and that they have other choices at their disposal.

'What may have been more effective' – this is powerful because you can make the feedback specifically about your character. Rather than stating that their default communication style is probably generally not working, you can share that it wasn't the most effective approach for your character. And again, you have the powerful neutral approach of framing it as an option rather than a rule.

'This is the stuff you have for free' – this is my go-to when delivering positive feedback. I share with them the communication areas they don't have to worry about, which seem natural or intuitive to them. It can also soften developmental feedback. So, I may say something like:

> You have excellent eye contact and incredibly open body language; that is the stuff you have for free. They both positively impacted me during the role play, as they calmed me down and made me feel safe sharing my story with you.
>
> You may want to pay more attention to your active listening skills. A few times during the conversation, you changed the subject when I indicated that I still wanted to talk about the subject we were on.

If they disagree with or challenge my feedback, I let them finish their point, breathe and then tell them it is okay. I say that I know it wasn't their intention for me to feel how I felt, but that was the impact on me. During some feedback sessions, I have had to repeat this a few times to the delegate as they continued to justify their actions. This can be for a variety of reasons; they may feel guilty, embarrassed or that they are right. Regardless, I stay firm with my statement as they cannot tell me how I felt.

I try not to use 'good' or 'bad' when delivering feedback. In my experience, as soon as you use the word 'good', they are just sitting there, not listening, waiting for the thing you are about to say that is 'bad'.

'Effective' is probably the safest and most neutral word to use. I will often refer to a behaviour as being effective or less effective.

Using 'liked' and 'loved' is okay when delivering positive feedback.

You may be able to take feedback notes during a role play, but I would try to get into the habit of not doing this. It can distract you from the role play and may not be appropriate for your character. You'll be surprised how much feedback you can retain as your experience grows.

# PART FOUR

# THE DIFFERENT TYPES OF ROLE PLAY

# CHAPTER TWENTY

# Pre-briefed role play

A pre-briefed role play does what it says on the tin: it thoroughly briefs the role play actor ahead of the job. It will contain all the information the actor needs to convincingly play the role and make it the most helpful learning experience for the participant or candidate. As I said earlier, role play briefs can vary massively in size and detail. Some role play briefs are overwritten and may contain unnecessary backstories and details. Remember that the person who has written the brief may not be an actor, so they will not know precisely what you, the role play actor, needs. Of course, take all the information on board, but remember that your job is to embody the behaviours within the brief. It is not to suddenly become an expert in banking, policing or international trade.

It's been nearly 20 years that I have worked in this field. I still get that same shudder before stepping over the corporate threshold that goes something like '... but I understand so little about *secondary investments*, I've never knowingly *synergised* anything with anyone, I have no idea what my *bandwidth* is and if can I *leverage* anything. And yet, after every delivery, I leave with the same sense of fulfilment that goes along the lines of "... of course, we brought something new to the party. Yes, we made an impact, it felt good to see our practical input pay dividends and, duh, more than a lightbulb or two went off when I offered my feedback ...." Once our client research is done, we can trust that we bring huge

> value to how the corporate world behaves and communicates. It
> does help to chuck in an acronym or a bit of jargon to be viewed as
> convincing though!'
>
> Tor Clark
> Actor

I read the brief thoroughly once and then go back through it
and highlight or note down what I feel are the most important
things for me to be able to do my job. You may need to look up
specific phrases, terminology or processes, but don't get bogged
down with this. Remember that the role play is to practise or
assess the participant's communication skills, not their technical
knowledge.

It is worth storing and keeping your briefs as jobs often come
around again. You may also have extra notes that you took
throughout the day that may be useful next time.

You may be the only person carrying out that particular brief on
that day, or there may be a team of role play actors playing the same
character. If there is more than one of you, it is worth checking in
with the other role players at the start of the day to ensure you are
all on the same page and delivering the same character and level of
challenge. The role plays won't, and shouldn't, be complete carbon
copies of each other, but the learning experience should be the same
for each participant. Once again, this is incredibly important if it is
an assessment role play.

If there is also a delegate brief, make sure you read that thoroughly
so you are aware of the information they have before they come in
and role play with you. The chances are that they will get their brief
on the day as opposed to you, who should have your role player
brief at least two weeks before a job.

If you are working with a facilitator, trainer or assessor and are
doing the role play more than once, I would check in with them
after your first role play to see if they would like you to adjust
anything or do anything differently.

Remember to ask the role play company for clarification if
anything in the brief does not make sense or is unclear. People make
mistakes sometimes, so it may not be you who has got it wrong,
and you may have highlighted an important error ahead of the day.

PRE-BRIEFED ROLE PLAY EXAMPLE ONE
FEEDBACK CONVERSATION ROLE PLAY
TRAINING ROLE PLAY

## Participant brief

You are about to meet Jay, one of your direct reports. Both you and Jay work in the customer service department of KNG Broadband. KNG Broadband is the second largest internet provider in Europe. KNG recently bought one of its smaller rivals FutureForce. FutureForce had a large customer base and was known for delivering good reliable internet speeds but had a reputation for terrible customer service. Various internet review sites have highlighted this, but it all came to a head last year when a call between a customer and a rude staff member went viral. FutureForce lost a lot of customers because of this incident.

KNG has always prided itself on its excellent customer service, which has become even more critical now that they have FutureForce's customer base.

Due to the buying of FutureForce and the increased pool of staff, there was some minimal restructuring, with a slight adjustment in some roles and reporting lines, but this didn't massively affect your team.

Jay works in your team in the customer care team division. Jay has worked for you for a year, and you feel they deliver adequate customer service. Jay is not one of the top performers and often needs feedback after calls of theirs that you have listened to.

A customer recently complained that they felt rushed by Jay and that Jay was condescending during a recent call. They also said there was a lot of background noise during the call, so it was hard to hear what Jay said. Jay is not aware of this complaint.

The customer care team at KNG Broadband can work two days a week from home, provided they can deliver the same level of customer service as they would in the office.

You have noticed that Jay has worked from home three days a week over the last three weeks and not the agreed two days a week.

It has been a while since you've had a one-to-one with Jay, so you want to have a general check-in and share the feedback from the recent customer complaint.

You also need to make Jay aware that if they cannot deliver the same level of customer service when working from home, they will have to work from the office full-time.

You have twenty minutes to have this discussion with Jay.

At the end of the twenty minutes, you and the actor playing Jay will discuss how the conversation went, and the actor will share their feedback.

## Role player brief

Your name is Jay, and you work in the customer care team for KNG Broadband. Previously you worked in the customer service department of a large insurance company. You worked there for five years but became increasingly frustrated with feeling like a number rather than a human being. The company was growing incredibly fast, and the culture was changing with it and, in your opinion, not for the best. You were really excited when you joined KNG Broadband. Even though they are Europe's second biggest broadband provider, the company culture felt like that of a smaller, friendlier business.

Since the acquisition of FutureForce, you have started to feel that things are changing at KNG. There are more people in the team now, and you have found some of the behaviours of some of the new staff members challenging, particularly Sophie, who is at the same level as you but has started to speak to you as if she is managing you. You feel that this is because Sophie was a team leader at FutureForce, but this is no longer the case now that she works for KNG. You think that you have noticed Sophie ignoring and avoiding phone calls. This is creating resentment from you and other team members.

The office vibe is changing, and it now feels incredibly cramped. You are starting to find yourself in a bad mood when in the office and have noticed that you have been short or impatient with a few customers.

You are finding that you prefer more and more to work from home. You feel you are more productive and happier and are not being distracted by other staff members avoiding doing their fair share of work.

Your neighbour at home had extensive building work last Wednesday, and you informed customers at the start of every call. However, you did not let anyone in the office know that this was the case.

You are fairly confident but can shut down or become quiet if you feel accused of anything.

If the delegate handles you correctly and seems genuinely curious about how things are for you at work at the moment, you will open up about the culture change, why you prefer working from home, how you feel about Sophie and share that you are worried about your future at KNG if it loses the company culture you used to enjoy.

If the delegate does not seem curious about your feelings and doesn't inquire about your side of things, you will become defensive. You will not share much information with them and will hint that this may no longer be the right company for you.

## PRE-BRIEFED ROLE PLAY EXAMPLE TWO
## SOCIAL WORKER ROLE PLAY
## ASSESSMENT ROLE PLAY

In this role play you will be playing the role of Ash, a fifteen-year-old child.

In reality, this conversation would take place over the phone, but for the purpose of the role play, you will sit back to back with the candidate.

There will also be an assessor in the room with you, who will sit in the corner of the room.

This assessment role play forms part of the recruitment process for social workers. As well as the role play, the candidates will have a written exam, interview and group activity with children.

It is your responsibility to manage the timings of this role play. This a ten-minute role play conversation. Nine minutes into the role play you must tell the candidate that you need to go as the school bell has gone. At ten minutes, you must end the call.

When the candidate is ready, they will start the call by saying *'Hello, Southampton Social Services, how can I help you?'*

## Ash's situation

Ash is fifteen years old and currently in year 10. They have a lot of schoolwork as they are preparing for their mock GCSE exams. Ash lives at home with their mother and younger sister Kay, who is eight years old. Ash's mother, Amanda, is a single parent and is currently doing a lot of overtime at work to support her family. Amanda is a security receptionist for an office building in central Southampton, and often works nights.

When Amanda is at home, she is often sleeping as she is so tired from work, and Ash feels like their mum often seems very sad. They have seen her cry a few times. Because Amanda is working so much Ash is having to do more at home for themselves and Kay. Ash picks Kay up from school every day and is doing a number of household chores. Ash is really stressed as they feel like they do not have enough time to do all of their school work. They miss their friends and the school choir club that they used to attend.

Ash knows that their mum is doing her best and that she feels bad that she is not at home a lot at the moment, so Ash doesn't want to bring how they are feeling up with her, as they know it will add to her stress.

Ash doesn't know what to do. They looked online last night and read some stuff about social workers and wondered if calling them might be a good idea.

Amanda has always had a very negative attitude towards social workers. Amanda's mum was also a single parent and was an alcoholic, so Amanda and her siblings were often taken away by social services when her mum needed recovery time. Amanda has always told Ash social workers tear families apart.

Ash loves their mum and sister and does not want their family torn apart but feels that they can't continue like this without burning out.

## Playing the role of Ash

Ash is very nervous about this call and will be hesitant and scared at the beginning of the call. It is up to the candidate to settle Ash's nerves and reassure Ash that making this call was the right thing to do and that the intention of social services is not to tear their family apart. Even if, as Ash, you are unhappy with the call, you must stay on it so the candidate can be assessed, but you can indicate to the candidate how you feel about the call.

## PRE-BRIEFED ROLE PLAY EXAMPLE THREE
## MEDICAL ROLE PLAY
## ASSESSMENT ROLE PLAY

## Role player instructions

Ten-minute role play

An examiner will be with you throughout the day and you will be role playing with twenty-four candidates in total.

Female identifying actor required

Character's name: Jennifer Harper

Age: twenty-four years old

You are in a very concerned state. You are overwhelmed by what has happened to you and you want answers and clarification from the doctor as soon as possible. A good candidate will acknowledge and address these emotions but will not allow you to force them into giving you a diagnosis before they have all of the information.

This morning you woke up in a good mood and had breakfast. At nine am you started to feel strange. You felt progressively worse and then collapsed. The next thing, you woke up in your hallway with a cut head. You have been incontinent of urine but not faeces. You have a pounding headache, but other than that you feel fine. Your speech and movement have not been affected.

No one has ever mentioned epilepsy to you. You did collapse a few months ago, but you did not go to the doctor or hospital.

You drink roughly seven cans of beer each day and smoke fifteen cigarettes per day.

You work in a dark kitchen preparing high-end delivery meals. You work long hours as you are trying to save up for a mortgage. You are stressed, feel overworked and tired. You have found that you are drinking more and more. You and your colleagues often start drinking as your work shift comes to an end.

You want to know what has happened to you, and whether it will happen again.

You feel it is vital that you leave this conversation with this information.

You start the conversation in an anxious state.

Please start each role play with the opening line:

> 'Oh Doctor! I am so stressed. I am so worried. I need some answers!'

At the end of each role play you will have five minutes to discuss how the candidate made you feel during the role play. During this time the examiner will also score and assess the candidate.

# CHAPTER TWENTY-ONE

# Forum theatre

'I 'd been working on a regular job with the same actor for some time. We got up to do our Forum Theatre scene, and he just went rogue. Shouting, getting in my face, spittle flying in my direction. I could see he was getting his acting rocks off, while I was just thinking "What the actual f*"£ is he doing?'

Turns out he'd gone to see a Hollywood actor on the West End the night before, and had been 'really inspired'. Needless to say, afterwards the facilitator gently reminded him this was a Diversity and Inclusion workshop, not the Garrick!'

Shelley Davenport
Role Player

Brazilian theatre director Augustus Boal created forum theatre. It is one technique that falls under the Theatre of the Oppressed umbrella term. This relates to the engagement of spectators influencing and engaging with the performance and with the power to stop and change it. It encourages audience interaction and explores different solutions for problems or issues.

Forum theatre is probably one of the first forms of role play work you will do and come across. It is an excellent introduction to the work, used a lot and may feel the closest to the traditional acting style you are used to.

Forum theatre places the delegates lived experiences on stage. It is an opportunity for them to view themselves and their environment from the position of an observer. It is used extensively in drama-based training as it is a safe way to explore themes and ideas with delegates. It is cost-effective; I have been part of forum theatre sessions for ten delegates and even up to one hundred delegates. Role play actors will always play the characters in the forum theatre scene, never the delegates. There is a chance that delegates may partake in the re-run of the forum theatre scene, but more on that later.

The role play company will have designed the forum theatre piece for a specific client's needs at that particular time. Forum theatre is a great way to tackle contentious and possibly emotion-stirring subjects such as racism, bullying, biases and cultural awareness. The role play company will have done much research, speaking to several people working at their client's company to ensure the piece is relevant and as accurate to life as possible. Often, the actual words the characters speak are from the anonymous mouths of staff members.

Forum theatre scenes can have two or more characters. It may be a one-to-one meeting, a larger group meeting or highlighting a fictional moment in an office setting. Generally, role play companies will play it safe and not set the forum theatre scene in the client's actual world or office but in a parallel, similar one so that the delegates empathize with the characters and recognize the behaviours and interactions they see on stage.

The actors can perform the forum theatre scene on an actual stage or raised platform, but it will often be in a meeting room or office. The session may occur on the client's premises or in a dedicated training venue like a hotel. No matter the environment, your role will always be the same.

Forum theatre scripts can vary but should be at most four or five pages long. Enough time to allow the audience to get to know the characters and observe the issues. It is worth remembering that it is a device to stimulate learning and generate discussion instead of conventional entertainment theatre.

A forum theatre scene will present a situation where things are not going well, where the staff members are not working well together or respecting one another. The scene will generally be a slightly heightened version of reality to bring it to life. Humour is often laced into forum theatre scripts, as it is a great way to put the audience at ease, help them relate to the scene, and empathize with the characters. This humour will probably contain a few in-jokes that may not make sense or land with you, but they will be a known part of the delegate's working world.

## How it works

The facilitator will introduce the audience to the scene and characters. One of the characters may also have the dual role of facilitating, but this would never be you if you are early on in your role play career.

One of the characters may deliver a monologue to the audience, sharing what is going on for them and their challenges. This monologue will set the scene for what the audience will see.

The forum theatre scene is played out.

At the end of the scene, the facilitator may 'thought/mind tap' the characters and ask them how they are feeling at the end of the scene. This will require the actors to share with the audience what emotions their characters are currently experiencing.

The facilitator will ask the audience to share their observations on the scene. They may ask questions such as:

*'What did you just observe?'*
*'What stood out most in the interaction you just witnessed?'*
*'What concerned you about what you just saw?'*

This will generally lead to a broader discussion around acceptable and unacceptable behaviours in their particular work environment.

After hearing these observations from the audience, the audience may get to 'hot seat' the characters to ask them questions. This is a chance for the audience to get under the characters' skin and discover what is happening for the character. It is an excellent chance for the audience to try empathizing with the characters, particularly those they may not have initially liked. If the audience is hot seating your character, you will have always rehearsed this with the facilitator, or it will be made clear in your brief what they want you to say and how they want you to respond to the audience.

The facilitator then informs the audience that they are now in control. They are now in charge of the scene and will be the directors and writers. The facilitator shares that the scene will start again from the beginning, and every time the audience sees something the characters do that they don't like, they have to shout, 'Stop!' This shouting of the word 'stop' will freeze the action. The audience member who shouts 'stop' will give directions to the characters, specific words and actions they would like the characters to say and do. The actor then takes this on board, and the scene moves forward. The facilitator tells the audience that if they don't shout 'stop', they will get a re-run of the original 'bad' version of the scene.

The audience will probably not be able to give this new direction to all the characters, but often only to the character who represents them. In the role play industry, we call this character the 'controllable character,' the character the audience can control. This character will typically be an embodiment of the audience. For example, the controllable character would be a manager if the audience is full of managers on a training course. If it was an audience of midwives and the scene was with a midwife and a patient. The controllable character would be the midwife. The idea is that we can only control ourselves and not other people. Still, if we change our behaviour and make it more effective, we may be able to influence the behaviour of others.

The scene will continue moving forward, hopefully coming to better outcomes. It is unlikely that the scene will conclude. This is fine, as it is not the point of the exercise. The point is to explore what happens in an interaction when we adjust the characters' behaviour and communication styles. As actors, you will start by following the script but naturally need to improvise as you receive new direction from the audience.

As the scene progresses and the audience becomes more comfortable and confident with being in charge of the action, the facilitator may invite one or two of them to take the place of the controllable character and deliver a message or line to the other character/s. This is an excellent opportunity for them to step into the character's shoes and see how it feels to deliver the message. It can often be easy for them to advise from the safety of being an audience member, but it can feel very different when they are in the hot seat. When I facilitate forum theatre sessions, I don't do this too often, as it can derail the scene if the delegates take it too far off track. The facilitator and team of actors will always have the learning objectives in mind so that they will keep the scene within the desired parameters. Although I may not get audience members up on stage often, I do often get them to interact with the character from the safety of their audience member chair.

At the end of re-running the scene, the facilitator may again 'thought/mind' tap and ask the characters how they are feeling. Hopefully, they will feel a lot better than they did at the end of the first run of the scene. This is also an opportunity for the character to give the audience feedback and share the most helpful advice offered to them and the other character/s during the forum theatre process.

Forum theatre is generally an enjoyable learning experience. The audience often buys into the drama and wants it to continue. It is usually a new learning method for them, and they get a lot out of it. It is an excellent opportunity to observe the power of this type of learning and watch your fellow role play actors and the facilitator in action. I have learnt so much this way over the years.

Forum theatre scenes are usually always rehearsed in advance; this may be ahead of or on the day. You will rehearse the 'bad' version and may rehearse what the 'good' version should hopefully look like or at least talk it through. The actors and facilitators must be on the same page regarding a forum theatre session. You should be clear on the learning objectives, why the forum scene was designed, and what the facilitator wants the delegates to get out of the session. Another reminder that you are always there for the benefit and learning of the delegates.

Forum theatre can be scripted or contain bullet points to improvise around. I will now share two examples of the type of forum theatre scene you may encounter.

All of the points I shared with you in 'How to do corporate role play' still apply, but in forum theatre, these skills are deployed by you opposite other fictional characters, as opposed to opposite participants.

Forum theatre characters often have gender-neutral names so that any actor of any gender can play them.

## FORUM THEATRE EXAMPLE 1

TRAINING PURPOSE: This scene has been designed for a manager training programme at a large multinational bank. The key skills the managers will explore on the programme are:

Leading with empathy
Active listening
How to have a coaching conversation with those they manage

The forum theatre scene will look at what can happen when we don't do this and what the consequences may be.

## CHARACTERS:

### Controllable character

**Manager:** Toby, mid-fifties. Investment banker. Has worked for Lion Banking for twenty-five years. It was his first job out of college, and he has worked his way up from the bottom. Very proud that he learnt the job on the ground. He is incredibly talented in the technical aspects of his job but does struggle with his interpersonal skills. He has always been managed by people who have a 'just get on with it' attitude and has adopted the same management style himself. He struggles with those who bring their feelings to work. Toby is incredibly overworked and is struggling to keep up with his work load and what is needed to manage his team.

### Non-controllable character

**Junior staff member:** Jo/Joe, mid-thirties. Analyst. Jo has worked for Lion Bank for five years and has worked in Toby's team for nine months. Jo is incredibly good at their job, detail focused and a well-respected member of staff. While working in Toby's team, Jo has to work very closely with Kevin, another analyst in the team. Kevin is older than Jo, and Jo is finding him more and more difficult to work with. Kevin is incredibly dismissive of Jo and has taken to now not responding to Jo's emails in a timely fashion. When he does, his emails are blunt, bordering on rude. Jo feels that Kevin is intimidated by their work and progression within the firm. Kevin and Toby have worked together for a number of years.

## Facilitator shares with audience:

The scene takes place in Toby's office. Jo has scheduled the meeting with Toby.

The meeting opens with Toby on the phone to Mark, another investment banker.

**Toby** *Mark! I know, I know, there is not much we can do about it. They are the client and what they say goes, I'm afraid. Yes, yes, I know, I know, we are all stretched, but we all know, what Simmons want, Simmons gets. Just think of the bonus ... We'll get there, we just may have to shift a few other things around ...*

Jo knocks on Toby's door. It is apparent that Toby had forgotten that this meeting was taking place today. Toby waves Jo in and indicates for them to sit down. He continues his phone call. Jo looks uncomfortable and uncertain.

**Toby** (still on the phone to Mark) *Yep, yep, ok let's look at doing that. Look, why don't I call you back in a bit, and we can formulate a plan and get both of our best people onto it. Yep, look, I have to go, I just need to have a quick one to one with one of the team. No, no, honestly, it won't take long. Speak in a bit. Bye, bye.*

(now talking to Jo) *Jo, Jo, sorry about that. It's been full on today and Mark is throwing his toys out of the pram.*

**Jo** *Erm, ok, sorry to bother you with this. We can reschedule if we need to*

**Toby** *No, no you're here now. Hit me!*

**Jo** *Erm, erm, ok, well thank you for taking the time, I really appreciate it, I know how busy you are at the moment*

**Toby** (cutting her off) *I think busy is here to stay Jo, I think I've been "busy for the last three years ..."*

**Jo** *Erm, yes, yes, quite. Ok I won't take long, I just wanted to erm ... check in, catch up ... get your thoughts ... I'm just* (Jo trails off as they lose confidence in articulating their thoughts).

The few seconds of silence panics Toby

**Toby**  *Ok, Jo, well thanks for coming, while you, erm, gather your thoughts, can I ask what capacity you might have to jump on board the Simmons project for a few weeks. They've moved the goal posts, again, and Mark has gone into meltdown. Probably looking at half a day a week if I can pull the right team together. Between you and me, I don't even think we should be having to put so much effort into this; it is primarily Mark's client, but he's saying that half his team are off on maternity, parental leave or whatever we're meant to call it nowadays, I mean don't even get me started on that!*

Jo looks confused and as if they don't know what to say. They nod along to Toby as he speaks, but their body language indicates that they just want the meeting to end.

**Toby**  *Sorry, sorry, I've gone off on the Toby train again. Let's crack on. Have you got a problem? Is it project Sapphire? Is the client not providing the deliverables you need?*

**Jo**  *Ah, no, project Sapphire seems to be ticking along ok ... I, I wanted to speak to you about something else. It's to do with the project I am working on with Kevin, well in particular ...*

Toby cuts Jo off while they are speaking

**Toby**  *Ah yes, of course, I forgot you are doing that too! Bloody hell you are busy. Tricky, tricky client, but I have known Pete who heads up the client team for years now. We play the occasional round of golf together, if you're dealing with any tricky characters on his side I can make a phone call for you.*

**Jo**  *Erm, no, no that won't be necessary. It was more to do with ... Actually, you know what, I think it's fine. I think it will sort it's self out. It's not a big deal.*

**Toby**  *Ok, ok, are you sure? We've probably still got a couple of minutes on the clock.*

**Jo**  (Getting up) *Yes, yes, it's fine. Thank you for your time today, Toby.*

**Toby**  *That is no worries at all, Jo; it is always a pleasure to catch up and see how things are going on the ground. Let's have another catch up soon and don't forget, my door is always open.*

**Jo**   *Ok, yes, yes, thanks Toby. Bye.*

**Toby**   (Going back to his phone) *Thanks Jo.*

## MINDTAPS

The facilitator asks both of the characters how they are feeling; the characters cannot hear each other when they share these thoughts with the audience:

**Jo**   *I am so annoyed. That was a disaster. Why couldn't I pull myself together? So typical of Toby, he just talks at you and it is so difficult to get a word in. I don't know what to do. I am really struggling at the moment and really need to find clarity. I was hoping that this would be a springboard for that, but once again, brick wall. I don't know what to do, things aren't going to change here, when it comes to these types of personalities. Maybe it's time to move one ...*

**Toby**   Yeah fine, it was good to see Jo. They've looked a little stressed of late, so it's good to know that they are not getting any trouble from Pete's team, as they're a bit 'old school'. I mean, I think there might be something going on, I did ask, but didn't get much back. Hopefully, they'll come and see me again or maybe they worked it out. Who knows with that generation ...

## RE-RUN OF THE SCENE

When the scene is re-run, if the audience get Toby to shift his behaviour, up his level of empathy and probe Jo in the right way, Jo will reveal:

> That they are really struggling to work with Kevin, as he is rude to them both in-person and via his email communication.
>
> Kevin is not sharing key documents with them, which is delaying the progress of the project.
>
> Kevin spoke over them three times during a recent client meeting.
>
> If things don't change with Kevin, they think they will have to leave the team or even the bank as his behaviour is starting to affect their mental health and confidence at work.
>
> They want Toby to speak to Kevin about his behaviour and maybe for all three of them to have a conversation that Toby facilitates.

## FORUM THEATRE EXAMPLE 2

**TRAINING PURPOSE:** This forum scene has been designed for Next Link Limited. Next Link Limited manage several serviced offices across the UK. Various types of companies rent their offices. Next Link's staff manage and maintain the buildings and offices. Next Link's management feel that staff are not collaborating well and wants them upskilled in empathy, listening, curiosity and maintaining boundaries.

**SETTING:** This scene takes place in Moorgate Tower—an organization similar to Next Level. Moorgate Tower is a 30-floor building in London with various types of tenants across their floors. This meeting is about some essential lift maintenance work which needs doing and the impact of that on the tenants and Moorgate Tower staff members.

# CHARACTERS:
## Controllable character

Melanie, Receptionist, mid-forties
   Melanie has worked on the main reception at Moorgate Tower for sixteen years. She has seen it all and feels that maintenance projects often get dragged out and become overcomplicated. Melanie wants the lift work to happen at a weekend as she feels it will cause too much disruption during the week.

## Controllable character

Carl, Facilities Manager, mid-fifties
   Carl has only been in the job for six months, having previously worked in facilities for a major hotel chain. Carl has become aware of many inefficiencies at Moorgate Tower and feels they have wasted money over the years not doing projects efficiently. Carl wants the lift work to happen during the week as the cost of the contractors, and having the building open at the weekend is very expensive. He also feels that if it doesn't occur during the week of the third of April, they may be in danger of voiding their insurance.

# Non-controllable character

Toni/Tony, Reception Manager at Tune Arm, thirties (Moorgate Tower's number one tenant, they rent six floors).

Toni is very busy and does not have time for this meeting. There is a lot of restructuring happening at Tune Arm, and they feel that they should be working with the Tune Arm executive team on that and not dealing with issues that the building management should handle. Toni has already cancelled one of these meetings. Toni is adamant that the lift work cannot happen the week of the third of April, as Tune Arm are hosting some of their top clients in their offices that week.

## *Scene*

The meeting opens with Carl on the phone to his partner. They seem to be upset, and Carl seems to be calming them down.

Melanie walks in and sits down. She notices that Carl is on a personal call and seems frustrated by this.

Carl ends his call and starts to work away on his laptop; something is clearly bothering him. He doesn't say hello to Melanie; they both sit working in silence.

Melanie eventually asks Carl if he received the email from Harriet about needing the budget forecasts.

Carl snaps at Melanie and says it is on his to-do list, which is growing by the minute.

Melanie tells Carl they are all busy and that he isn't the only one.

Carl says he can't believe that Toni is late again; he says they are just wasting time and need a decision on the lift situation today.

Melanie says that Toni is a customer and we can't do anything about them being late. She says that the lift decision is obvious, and minimal disruption is needed to maintain the office's professionalism.

Toni walks in and says they had a mess up with their calendar and thought this meeting was happening tomorrow.

Carl cuts Toni off while they are speaking and says they must decide on the lifts today. He then gives a detailed explanation of why it must happen during the week of the third of April. He doesn't notice that both Melanie and Toni seem not to be listening to him. It is apparent in their body language.

Melanie loses her temper and tells Carl he is not the only one in the meeting with an opinion. She says that having the works during the week will not be acceptable. She says it will disrupt too many people, and she'll be dealing with the complaints all week.

Toni stands up and says that they don't care if it is the week or the weekend; it just can't happen the week of the third of April due to the hosting of clients. They say they need to go and feel the building management team should be sorting this out, not rent-paying tenants.

There is an awkward silence.

Melanie apologies for bothering Toni and says that she and Carl will sort this out and promises that the work will not take place during the week of the third of April.

Carl says that is unacceptable and that the three of them must talk it through now. He tells Toni they need to be part of the decision-making process as they occupy so many floors at Moorgate Tower.

Melanie's phone rings.

Carl asks everyone to put their phones on silent so they can focus.

Melanie says that that is rich for Carl to say, considering he was on the phone sorting out his dinner plans when she walked in.

Carl goes to say something but stops himself. He looks really upset. He asks them to excuse him momentarily, and he leaves the room.

Both Melanie and Toni are left in stunned silence.

After the delegates have a short discussion about the scene, it will be re-run to try and bring it to a better conclusion. The delegates will be able to direct and coach the characters of Carl & Melanie.

# CHAPTER TWENTY-TWO

# Bespoke role play

Bespoke role play, also known as practice conversations or real play, is the newer and increasingly popular form of role play.

The participant gets to practise a real conversation with a role play actor and then receive feedback on their communication skills. To be clear, you will play the person the participant wants to have the conversation with, and the participant will be themselves having it. The conversation can be any chosen by the participant. It might be a conversation they had in the past that they want to re-run to a better conclusion, a current conversation they need to have with a colleague or one they feel they may need to have in the future. Generally, bespoke work requires more time and takes place in small groups, making it more expensive for the client. Bespoke sessions may be one role player to one participant or one role player working with up to three participants, practising a conversation with each participant. The beauty of the group session is that the participant doesn't only learn from being in the hot seat, practising their conversation, but they also get to observe and potentially provide their colleagues with feedback on their practice conversations with the role play actor.

Bespoke role play is a more advanced form of role play than pre-briefed and forum theatre, and one you are unlikely to touch in your first couple of years. Bespoke requires you to be more of an actor facilitator than a role play actor because of the way you need to facilitate the feedback, especially if you are working with a small group.

Whether working in a small group or one-to-one, you must ensure that the participants feel safe. They may feel incredibly vulnerable before practising a real-life conversation. I have had a handful of participants cry during bespoke sessions. It is courageous of them to practise such a conversation with a stranger, and they need to believe that they are in a safe space with a professional neutral role play actor. The kind, caring, centred behaviour that I said is required for feedback sections is imperative in a bespoke session.

Bespoke sessions can be anything from twenty minutes up to an hour long.

I don't think you have to play a character with the same gender identity as you in a bespoke role play. This is because it is all about embodying behaviours. A brief may specifically mention the gender of someone, or it may be crucial for a participant to have an actor of a particular gender, but I find that these occasions are rare.

I always start my bespoke sessions by introducing myself and providing some personal background. Building this level of trust and buy-in at the start of the session is important. I then do what I call 'contract confidentiality'; this is essentially an agreement that what happens in the room stays in the room. This is more important if it is a group bespoke session. Remember that, if the delegates work in the same organization, you may be playing someone known to the other participants, so contracting this level of confidentiality is very important.

It's easy to get trapped inside what is the dramatic or fun way for a character to behave in a certain situation but the biggest lesson for me was connecting to the needs of the participant in the practice conversation. Where can I challenge them more if they're doing well? Where can I tone down the strength of my responses, if necessary? What would allow them to stretch themselves, particularly in the areas they wish to develop? As the session unfolds it's these kinds of questions that allow me to continuously calibrate the best practice for that specific individual.'

Mason Philips
Facilitator and Role Player

I then share that this is an opportunity for them to practise a high-stakes conversation in a low-stakes environment. It is a safe space, and there are no consequences if they, in their eyes, get it wrong. It is a chance to be brave, to potentially try a different communication style from what they are used to.

Usually, the participant will have filled in a pre-session questionnaire before the session containing all of the conversation details. You should have received this in plenty of time to digest the character and the situation. The level of detail on the form will vary massively, so you may have to ask the participant some additional questions before the bespoke role play. Your job here is to get as much information as possible to convincingly play the person on the form. You may also find that the form contains a lot of technical or business information and not enough behavioural things that apply to the character you will be playing; again, if this is the case, you will need to pull this information out of the participant.

Before we start, I always ask the participant if they would prefer to refer to me using the person's name or use my name. Sometimes they appear to feel safer when they can use mine.

There is every possibility that they won't have filled in the form ahead of the session. They may have forgotten, been too busy or are concerned about putting something so personal to them on an online questionnaire. If this is the case, you can get everything you need in a five-minute conversation before you dive into the role play.

They may arrive at the session and inform you that they no longer want to practise what is on the form but a different conversation. This is fine; we, as role players, go with it. What is most important is that the participant practises the most helpful conversation for them to practise, and that may have changed since they filled in the form.

I let them know that if they see me taking any notes during the role play, these are for the feedback conversation we will have afterwards.

Once I am clear about who I am playing, what the participant needs to practise, and why, I am ready to begin the bespoke role. It is helpful to enter the scene as the character to show that you are now a new person. It might be a case of walking through the door, getting up and sitting back down, or if on a virtual platform, turning your camera off and back on again.

Generally, I wouldn't let the role play run for more than ten minutes. It will probably take them a few minutes to relax in the believability of the role play conversation. I tend to keep it going until I have seen enough of their communication challenges, the moments they are getting stuck on or what I would like to give them feedback on.

They may lose confidence and stop the role play. If they do this, I would stop, come out of character and check in with how they are feeling. Better to have a conversation about it and then try and dive back into the practice conversation.

If this hasn't happened, I will stop the role play when I have seen enough. I usually indicate this by using the time-out symbol. This is a perfect moment to deploy some of the feedback transition tools I mentioned in 'How to give feedback' to relax the participant and clarify that you are now back to being the actor facilitator and are no longer the character.

In a bespoke session, I have a rigid feedback structure that I stick to.

---

I first ask the participant:

*What did you do well during our conversation?*

I never ask them: How was that? Because they will start to give themselves a lot of negative feedback. Even when I ask them 'What did you do well during our conversation?' they will typically give themselves one piece of positive feedback and then list all the things they felt they could have done better. I am pretty strict with this; I keep pushing them to celebrate what they did well.

If there are other participants/observers in the room, I ask them the same question:

*What did they see the participant do well during the conversation?*

My second question to the participant is:

*What do you feel you could have done differently during our conversation?*

I am careful with my language here; I use the word differently because it is about choices instead of having done anything wrong.

If there are other participants/observers in the room, I once again ask them the same question:

*What do you feel the participant could have done differently during our conversation?*

I then share my feedback. I think the actor facilitator should always feedback last (as if they feedback too early); there is potential for them to influence what the participant and observers may say. I think it is also better for the participants to reflect on their behaviours and analyse why they may have communicated in the way they did. Also, going last means you have a chance to gather your thoughts while they are speaking.

I am careful with my feedback. I don't overload them; I give them gentle steers on what they did and its impact on me. I think it is okay if your feedback differs from or contradicts what has been feedback by the participant or observers. You were on the receiving end of their communication, so you may have experienced things differently.

'I find it helpful not being the first person to give feedback, as it gives me a chance to collect my thoughts, and, often, hearing other people's comments triggers my own memory, and I'm reminded of things where I was unable to make notes of my own.'

Robert Boulter

Actor

If time allows, I practise more with the participant. Before the second practice, I check in with the participant about my embodiment of the character. Is there anything they would like me to do more or less? Would they like me to be more or less challenging, or was it just right? Is there anything specific they would like me to say or do?

When we go back in, it might be a case of pinpointing a particular moment during the conversation to re-run and for them to implement the feedback they have received. It might be the beginning of the conversation, a crucial moment or the bit where they must deliver a difficult message. If it is an hour one-to-one bespoke session, you can do this a few times, feeding back after each mini-practice.

As you move through these mini-practice and secondary feedback conversations, it is worth checking in with the participant and asking how they feel. How do they feel when they shift their communication style? How does it feel if they speak slower, allow themselves time to breathe, embrace silence and actively listen?

Remember to reward their good behaviour. As you see them make shifts, reward, reward, reward. It may be the first time they have left three seconds of silence, maintained eye contact, stuck with the open questions, or deployed the QaQa technique. All things that can be transformational for their communication skills moving forward. This is the power of the work.

If it is a group bespoke session, I repeat the above process with each participant.

'Listen with your eyes as well as your ears, was a piece of invaluable advice I was given when I first started as a role player. I would diligently write down as much information as I could when a delegate was describing the conversation they wanted to practice. I didn't want to miss anything but what I later realised was that no amount of writing on a page would help me listen with my eyes and ears. So the next time I went into the training room I made a decision to stop writing and just listen, really listen.'

Julia Montague
Role Play Actor and Facilitator

Here are two examples of bespoke role play pre-session questionnaires.

## BESPOKE ROLE PLAY QUESTIONAIRE

### EXAMPLE 1

In the session you will have the opportunity to practise a challenging conversation with one of the role players. The role player will play the person you need to have the conversation with. After the conversation, the role player will give you feedback on how they felt during the conversation.

For the role player to portray your chosen person to the best of their ability they will need some background information on them and the situation. Please answer the following questions with as much detail as possible.

## Your name

Fahzana Sithy

## Why do you want to practise this conversation?

I need to have a challenging conversation with one of my colleagues, Max. We both work in the accounts department for a high street chain. Max and I have worked together for eight years and have always had a good working relationship. We had worked on many projects together, and I have always appreciated their knowledge as they have worked within the organization for twelve years.

## Which person/type of person would you like the role player to play?

Max

## What is the conversation about?

Three months ago our manager left and we both applied for their job. I got the job, so I am now Max's line manager. Since that happened I feel like our relationship has really changed. I no longer sit with the team, as I have an office. Max has contradicted me a few times during team meetings and makes jokes at my expense quite often. Max and I have never discussed (in any detail) me getting the job over them.

## What type of reaction do you expect from the person the role player is playing?

Very loud and confident character, often cutting people off when they are talking

## What sort of things might they say?

They say things like 'Look at you, up in your ivory tower.' 'I can see you've got your manager hat on again.' 'You're the manager, I thought you were supposed to have all of the answers.'

## How would you describe their body language?

very expressive

What is the best outcome for this conversation?

Clear the air with Max around me getting the job. Address what I think is some of the unnecessary banter about me being the manager now.

What is the worst outcome for this conversation?

Max gets defensive and aggressive.

Any other information?

No, thank you. I am nervous about practising this conversation, but I know it will help me.

'I am often struck by participants who say 'He is just like that!' or 'You are so like her!'. Of course the actors are embodying the behaviour, but there can also be a strong dose of projection on the part of the participant. It may be useful for the actor to remember that, like any audience member, participants play a significant role in the suspension of disbelief.'

Kath Burlinson
Theatre Director and Leadership Trainer

## PRACTICE CONVERSATION
## DELEGATE INFORMATION

### EXAMPLE 2

BELOW ARE THE DETAILS THAT THE DELEGATE HAS FILLED IN ABOUT THE CONVERSATION THEY NEED TO HAVE:

Name: Thomas Cartwright

I need to have a challenging conversation with one of my direct reports, Janet. Janet is a project team leader. I am a project manager for a large supermarket chain looking after new builds. Janet is responsible for one of our new Metro stores in Milton Keynes. A number of deadlines have been missed, and I have heard from some of those working in her team that they are struggling to work with her. Janet is a detail person who is meticulous about everything she does. When she was a team member this was fine, as her job role required it. But now that she is a team leader she needs to be able to manage more things which might mean sacrificing some detail. Or at least delegating some of this 'detailed work' to a member of her team.

Janet is quite a shy, introverted individual. She is very softly spoken and doesn't give particularly long answers when you ask her questions. She takes a long time to think of her answers, and this can be very frustrating. We work in such a fast-paced environment that no one really has time for this. I find myself sometimes finishing her sentences or summarising what I think she might say. I know that this isn't good 'management or leadership' but I am so busy. Janet will often say things like 'Oh, I had never thought of it that way' 'Oh, that's interesting, let me go away and think about it' – lots of ways of filling conversations with no actual answers.

I need to have a conversation with Janet about all of this and get her to pull her socks up. I am also aware that I need to give her time and space to let me know what is going on for her, but I find this quite difficult.

# CHAPTER TWENTY-THREE

# Virtual role play

As I previously shared, a great deal of role play work now happens on virtual platforms. In some capacity, hybrid working and virtual role play are here to stay.

There are many benefits to role play clients, including:

- Delegates and role players can be anywhere in the world.

- The sessions can accommodate staff who are working in different time zones.

- Sessions can be organized at short notice.

- The client doesn't have to provide lunch or pay for travel costs.

- You can train a lot more people virtually and split off into any number of smaller break-out rooms.

- Some delegates feel safer and less vulnerable practising difficult conversations virtually.

- Much of their employee's communication is now virtual, so it makes sense for them to practise these skills on the platform they will be using.

The benefits for us role players include:

- Not having to travel to and from the jobs.

- You can potentially squeeze in more jobs or rehearsals per day as you bounce from virtual call to virtual call. I think I managed four in a day once.

- You can work unsociable hours with delegates in different time zones if that suits you.

- If it is a long role play day, such as a medical role play day, you can find helpful ways to step away and reset between role play sessions.

- Very easy to squeeze a virtual audition into your day of virtual role playing.

All types of corporate role play can function on a virtual platform. Many sceptics at the start of the pandemic didn't think this to be the case, especially when it came to forum theatre; time has now dispelled this. It works just as well. Online will never be able to replicate the energy of an in-person training session entirely, but it is a close second and is still hugely impactful.

When preparing for an online role play session, please pay close attention to all of the virtual tips I shared with you in 'The audition' chapter:

- Looking into the webcam when speaking and at their face on the screen when listening to them.

- Have your light source behind you. Maybe invest in a cheap ring light to use when there is no natural light available due to the time of day.

- Make sure your webcam is in line with your eyes. You can achieve this simply by placing your laptop on a few large books. Remember, you don't accomplish this by tilting your laptop screen.

- Think about your framing; take up as much of the screen as possible and make sure you are centre.

Once again, you want to model the desired behaviours when you deliver on a virtual platform. You definetly should model these behaviours unless your character deliberately does not embody the above points because they feel scared, worried, upset or unsafe. If your character is not presenting the desired behaviours, it is helpful if you can adjust yourself back to a more neutral position as you move into the feedback section. You, the actor, should be modelling perfect virtual communication. Again, this is another helpful way to show the distinction between the character you are playing and you, the professional role play actor.

To role play virtually, you must ensure your internet connection is excellent and your computer is in good working order. I often reset my internet connection before a virtual job, so I know it works at its best.

Most virtual sessions take place on Zoom or Teams. If you aren't already, I suggest you get familiar with their basic functions. There are YouTube tutorials you can watch on this. No one will expect you to be a tech expert, but the facilitator and role play company will want you to feel and appear comfortable when delivering their work virtually. The role play company will organize a rehearsal beforehand if you need to do a specific technical thing for a particular job. If it is your first time working on a virtual platform, run a test call with a friend to ensure they can hear and see you well.

Most built-in computer microphones and speakers are adequate for virtual role play jobs, but it might also be worth purchasing a cheap headset as a backup.

I would also consider any background noise in your house, as this can make you appear unprofessional to the role play company and the participants. You want to find the quietest spot in your home. I even put a note on the door to remind those I live with that I am on an important virtual call. If your next-door neighbour decides to start building work unexpectedly, you cannot do much about that. Although I was once running a virtual session when such a thing happened, I popped outside on a break, spoke to the builders and then gave them my timetable. They agreed to do all the loud work during my breaks or when I could put myself on mute. Where there's a will, there's a way!

Virtual rehearsals and virtual briefing calls are common now for both virtual and in-person jobs. It is much easier to find a time and date that suits everyone when it is a virtual rehearsal or call.

Naturally, with it being virtual, you can log on from anywhere. I have done the odd virtual job while away on holiday or during my downtime when away on another role play or acting job. Ensure that you can maintain your professional set-up and that the internet connection is adequate.

Working virtually allows you to have some cheat or prompt sheets stuck up on the wall around you. I often do this when delivering virtually if there are key things that I need to remember.

Role play actors have become very good at convincingly reading their lines off the computer screen while delivering virtual forum scenes. Don't get me wrong: you still need to be incredibly familiar with the lines and the learning points, but it does take the pressure off you regarding line learning. You will need to play around with your desktop to see the script and the virtual session, but now all role players who deliver virtually do it, and it will not be obvious to the delegates. Some role players have the text on the screen and also stuck up beside their computer so they can be more mobile during the role play.

Your fee for a virtual job should be the same as if it were an in-person job. There might be a slight decrease depending on the job, the company and the client, but I don't think this should generally be the case. Roleplayers deliver the same quality of work, no matter the platform, so our fee should reflect this.

# CHAPTER TWENTY-FOUR

# Filmed role play

The filming of role play scenarios is very common. These will be specific films designed and written to assist in a particular piece of learning. You may film one version of a conversation or, like in forum theatre, an unsuccessful and best-practice version.

Having filmed scenes to play in training sessions is very cost-effective for clients and the films can be used for as long as they want to use them. The client is paying to use the film for internal training, or there may be an agreement to post it on their internal work intranet. The role play company should have made it contractually clear that the material should never find itself in the public domain. This is about your image, work and what will be available to anyone who googles your name. Have this conversation with the role play company; running it past your agent might also be worth it. If you want to be super cautious, let your agent handle it.

Once you agree to do the job, the role play company will send you the script and all the additional information you need. You may have a rehearsal beforehand, but that is unlikely. You will need to be off-book on the day of filming. Time is usually quite tight due to budget constraints, so they will need all actors to be on top of their lines on the day of filming. A word of warning: you may find corporate scripts more challenging to learn than the dialogue you are used to learning for TV and film work. The script must often contain specific information or jargon, which may not flow for you but will be essential for the film's learning points. Make sure you allow enough time to learn it, and as soon as you arrive on the day, grab any moment you can with your fellow actors to run the lines.

Again, you may be filming on location in the client's office or a dedicated studio.

Some filmed scenarios may involve you delivering a monologue or presenting to camera. If this is the case, you should have the option of using an autocue. Even if there is an autocue facility on the day, you should still be familiar with the lines. It is unlikely that autocue will be an option if it is an actual role play scene with you and other characters.

Your fee should be higher than what a role play company pays you for a typical role play day. The client is also paying for the usage of the material in the future, so this should be more of a buy-out situation, like in the world of commercials. I'm afraid it is not commercial world money but still an above-average wage for a day's work. Half a day should pay you around £400 and a full day around £600. In my experience you may be required to do one to four films in a day; remember, they are paying you for the day, not per line or film.

The role play company will generally ask you to provide your own wardrobe for corporate films. They should be clear on what they need you to bring; it is usually just a few options in different colours. The dress style will probably be close to what you would wear to a regular role play job.

It is unlikely that there will be any hair and make-up facilities on site. The film will probably be looking to recreate a realistic office environment.

Corporate role play filming is often fun and an excellent opportunity to practise for upcoming on-screen work and auditions.

No role play company, client or facilitator should ever spring on you last minute that they want to film a standard role play you are doing or a forum session you are part of. This is not acceptable and not what they are paying you for. You are perfectly within your rights to say no.

They may ask you if they can take some pictures of a session you are part of for internal purposes or their social media. Please use your discretion here; once again, it is your image. Nine times out of ten, it is harmless, and no one will see it. But if it goes out into the public domain, consider if you are happy to be associated with that client's brand or if you want your role play work visible to the wider world. I am not precious about my image and, obviously, am happy for the world to know that I do this work, but I always judge the picture question on a case-by-case basis.

# CHAPTER TWENTY-FIVE

# Final thoughts

Well done for making it to the end of the book; you have absorbed a lot of information. I now suggest you step back, get some fresh air and let all the information in the book settle.

As you move through your role play journey, it is a good idea to go back to the specific chapters which apply to you at that particular moment.

As I have said, you can start your role player learning journey from now:

- Up your level of curiosity in all aspects of your life.

- Notice in yourself and others what opens people up and closes them down during conversations.

- Start to tune into the types of questions you and others are asking.

- Imagine the type of feedback you would give someone after a conversation.

- Practise giving people feedback, using the 'When you' 'I felt' model – be strict with yourself – keep it evidence-based and not opinion-based.

- If you know someone else who has read this book, practise role playing and delivering feedback to them. In fact, search **#SyrusRPPractice** on social media to find others you can practise your role play and feedback skills with virtually or even in person, if you are local to each other.

Remember that every day is a school day, and a role play career is a marathon, not a sprint; it will take time, but with hard work and dedication, you will get there.

Yes, it is your skill, but also your reputation, which will get you reemployed. Be nice, be kind, be present and be proactive. These are the type of people we in the industry want to work with.

Good luck, and I hope to see you on a job soon, in person or virtually.

Syrus :-)

# INDEX